WEIGHT TRAINING
For Life

By

JAMES L. HESSON
Delta State University

MP

MORTON PUBLISHING COMPANY
925 West Kenyon Avenue, Unit 4
Englewood, Colorado 80110

First Edition
1 2 3 4 5 6 7 8 9

Printed in the United States of America

Contents

Acknowledgements

I would like to thank everyone who helped make it possible for this idea to become a reality. Special appreciation is given to the following individuals:

Bill Powell for his excellent photography, suggestions, hard work, and support.

Willie Brown, Debra Perry, and Medgar Scott for their time, effort, skill, and patience as models.

Tommy Burnham, Judy McNeece, and Ben Mitchell for computer access.

Dinah Hensarling for typing much of the original manuscript.

Dr. Tom Kidd and Dr. Phil Allsen for their inspiration and knowledge.

Dr. Milton Wilder and Dr. Lisso Simmons for their encouragement and for believing in me.

Mr. Doug Morton for the opportunity as well as for his kindness, courtesy, faith, encouragement, patience, and understanding.

Student Preface

This book has been written to help you. Learning about weight training can be difficult, confusing, and embarrassing. I hope that this book will make it simple and clear. This book does not include everything there is to know about weight training, but it will give you a good foundation of current factual information. This is a book for beginners, not for exercise physiologists or advanced strength athletes. Most of all, this is a book to help you get started weight training for life.

Teacher Preface

This book has been written to help you. Teaching weight training can be overwhelming or oversimplified; it can also be frustrating. This book does not attempt to cover everything you know about weight training, but it does attempt to cover some basic information that your beginning students need to know.

One big problem for many weight training teachers is time. Do you have enough class time to tell your students all that you wish you could about weight training? Are your students always present, on time, and alert for your weight training lectures? Do you have other classes to prepare for? Are yo paid for talking or for ensuring that learning takes place? Are you bored with presenting the same beginning information year after year? Could you be more productive if you did not have to repear the same basic information over and over? Would your students learn more effectively if they were required to actively seek information (which they could cover at their own speed and repeat as often as necessary) or passively listen to a one-time lecture? Do you have enough class time to present all of the information you want and still have enough exercise time? These questions refer to problems that we all face as weight training teachers.

This book is a tool that could help you perform your task of teaching weight training. It could make your performance of this task better, and at the same time, easier. A book will never replace you as a teacher because your role is much more dynamic and complex. Your responsibility is to create a stimulating learning environment, to provide motivation, to provide direction, and to provide feedback. I am sure this tool can be designed better if we work together. As you work with this book, let me know how we can improve it to help you and your students.

To my parents, Jack and Gladys Hesson, who taught me the basic values and attitudes that have made all other learning and accomplishment possible.

To all of the teachers and coaches who so freely gave me their time, effort, and knowledge.

To my wife and children, Margie, Jennifer, and David, for their love and support.

CHAPTER 1

Weight Training—What, Who, and Why

WHAT IS WEIGHT TRAINING?

Progressive resistance exercise is a form of exercise in which the resistance to the exercise movements is gradually and progressively increased. Weight training is one form of progressive resistance exercise in which "weights" of different sizes are added to or taken from the total load or resistance.

There are different reasons for performing weight training exercises. The following categories of weight trainers are based upon these differences.

WHO TRAINS WITH WEIGHTS AND WHY?

OLYMPIC LIFTERS. Olympic lifting is a competitive sport. The object in olympic style lifting competition is to see who can lift the most total weight overhead using two different lifts. The two olympic lifts are the snatch and the clean and jerk. The snatch lift requires that the weight be lifted in one continuous movement from the floor to a position in which the weight is above the head and both arms are straight. The lifter may drop below the weight to catch it overhead but must rise to a stationary standing position to complete the lift. In the clean and jerk the weight must first be brought from the floor to a position on the upper chest and shoulders, then it is thrust overhead to a straight arm finish. The winner is the individual with the highest total weight lifted when the two lifts are added together. Competitors are divided into body weight classifications so that the lifter with a body weight of 120 pounds does not have to beat a lifter with a body weight of 350 pounds to win.

POWER LIFTERS. Power lifting is another sport which involves competitive lifting. Power lifters compete in three lifts; the bench press, squat, and dead lift. The winner is the lifter with the highest total for the three lifts in that body weight classification.

ATHLETES. Since the rehabilitation work of Dr. Thomas DeLorme following World War II, progressive resistance exercise has gradually gained acceptance by the medical profession and the coaching profession. Most top-level athletes now use some form of weight training to improve their sports performance and to recover from injuries. Muscles are responsible for all human movement. Athletes who improve their muscular system usually improve their sports performance.

PATIENTS. Physicians and physical therapists prescribe progressive resistance exercise for people who have been injured to rebuild the muscular system. Patients regain strength, function, and muscle size after an injury by training with weights.

BODY BUILDERS. Body builders participate in competition that is more art than sport. Through the use of weight training they create human sculpture using human muscle as the clay. Body builders attempt to develop the maximum muscular size while maintaining a balanced appearance (symmetry) and a high degree of muscular visibility (definition). In this activity it is the appearance of the body that is most important.

PHYSICAL FITNESS ENTHUSIASTS. There is a rapidly increasing number of people who do not fit into any of the categories mentioned but who are discovering the benefits of training their muscular system. Most of these individuals are lifting weights so that they will look better and feel better. This book has been written primarily for the beginning weight trainer and the physical fitness enthusiast.

WEIGHT TRAINERS. Everyone who trains with weights.

SHOULD WOMEN TRAIN WITH WEIGHTS?

Is weight training an appropriate activity for women? Absolutely! There is nothing to be gained from physical weakness. A strong, healthy woman has an irresistible vitality and an aura of vibrant good health.

All women experience increases in muscular strength when they participate in heavy weight training programs. However, most women do not experience much increase in muscular size. This inability to gain muscle size is thought to be related to low levels of the male hormone testosterone and high levels of the female hormones.

Weight training will not make a woman appear masculine. Since women do show increases in strength with very little change in muscle size, the result is a strong, firm, shapely, healthy appearance.

The location and function of skeletal muscles is essentially the same in all humans, male or female. Therefore, weight training exercises are the same for men and women. There are no "men's exercises" or "women's exercises" in weight training. However, men and women may choose to concentrate upon the development of different body parts which may affect their selection of exercises.

WHO CAN BENEFIT FROM WEIGHT TRAINING?

Everyone who has a muscular system can benefit from a regular program of progressive resistance exercise. The primary benefits are improvements in strength, muscular endurance, and appearance.

ELEMENTARY AGE CHILDREN (ages 6 to 12). There is no indication that weight training is harmful to children.

However, until more evidence is available, it is probably wise to
have young children train with moderate to light weights that
can be handled for fairly high repetitions (at least 10 repetitions
or more) if they want to train at all. Obviously, if children are
forced to train at this young age they will not develop a very
good attitude to this beneficial activity. There is no need for
children to attempt maximum lifts using heavy weights. If
children are allowed to lift, they should have adult supervision.

JUNIOR HIGH SCHOOL (ages 12 to 15). After puberty and
during adolescence as hormone changes occur, children can
begin to experience their greatest physical changes or gains as a
result of a weight training program. Heavier weight and lower
repetitions may be performed as long as strict exercise form is
maintained. Close adult supervision is necessary at this age.
Boys this age seem to have an overwhelming urge to find out
who can lift the most weight.

HIGH SCHOOL (ages 15 to 18). As children near full growth
and full physical maturity, weight training can have a dramatic
positive effect on their physical performance, appearance, and
self-confidence. This is a time when they can handle heavier
exercise loads and more intense exercise programs. Still, weight
training must be performed correctly to maximize safety and
progress. The incorrect exercise technique to which some boys
resort in order to move a heavier weight can result in injury.
Weight training exercises performed correctly rarely result in
injury.

YOUNG ADULTS (ages 18 to 22). Young adults have
perhaps the greatest potential for physical development
whether they are training for strength, muscular endurance,
muscular size, or physical fitness.

MID-LIFE ADULTS (ages 22 to 65). Very little of the decline
in strength during these years is due to natural aging. In
societies that have a high degree of technology and automation,
there is a tremendous loss of strength and mobility during these
years due to inactivity. Many individuals who are in these
wage-earning years feel that they do not have time to exercise.

Weight training is a very efficient form of exercise because of the ability to isolate a muscle or muscle group and work it very hard in an extremely short period of time. A stimulus sufficient to elicit a gain in strength in a muscle may be achieved in less than one minute following some weight training programs. This is a greater strength gain stimulus than the same muscle would achieve in hours participating in most recreational activities. If your time for exercise is short, weight training is the fastest way to maintain or increase the functioning of the muscular system.

OLDER ADULTS (age 65 plus). Beyond an approximate age of 65, there appears to be a slightly more rapid decline in physical performance. It is very hard to tell how much of that decline is due to the decrease in physical activity that often accompanies retirement and the psychological decision that it is time to get old. It is important for those over 65 to maintain their muscular system if they wish to maintain their mobility. Muscular contraction is responsible for all human movement. Enjoyment is often closely related to physical mobility at all ages but becomes more obvious with older adults who have lost their ability to move around on their own.

WEIGHT TRAINING FOR LIFE. Weight training is an efficient form of exercise to develop and maintain the muscular system throughout life. Though your goals and training programs will change as you progress through life, weight training is a valuable lifetime activity that should be continued.

WHAT CONTRIBUTIONS CAN WEIGHT TRAINING MAKE TO TOTAL PERSONAL DEVELOPMENT?

Total personal development includes physical, mental, social, emotional, and spiritual development. Weight training can contribute to all of these areas.

PHYSICAL. Weight training makes its most obvious contributions to physical development. Strength, muscle endurance, and flexibility can all be developed and maintained through regular participation in a well-designed weight training program. Strength is developed by forcing a muscle to move a heavy resistance. Muscular endurance is developed by forcing a muscle to work against a moderate resistance for many repetitions. Flexibility is developed or maintained by performing such exercise movement through the full range of motion and by always exercising the opposing muscles.

MENTAL. A successful weight training program requires intelligent planning, consistent self-discipline, continual analysis, and insightful problem solving.

SOCIAL. Social qualities are developed when training is performed with others. Sharing, caring, and helping are among the positive social qualities that occur during a weight training workout. Weight training provides a time to participate together in an activity that produces positive results for all of the participants. Everyone is a winner in weight training, whereas many recreational games must result in a winner and a loser. Weight training provides a common activity in which to participate and to discuss as well as a time to be together. Weight training is an excellent activity for families or friends, since everyone can be together, yet each can perform their own training program at their own level without interfering with the progress of anyone else. Since a good weight training program includes the achievement of goals, there is a bond that develops among those who overcome difficult obstacles together.

EMOTIONAL. Weight training can help a person release emotional stress and tension. There is a measurable decrease in neuromuscular tension following a weight training session. There is also an opportunity to release anger and frustration in a socially acceptable manner—intense physical activity. Since weight training involves overcoming physical difficulties during each training session, some regular participants seem to adopt a more objective approach to other obstacles and difficulties in their lives, resulting in greater emotional stability.

SPIRITUAL. This is one of those intangible things that cannot be adequately measured or described. There is a feeling of inner peace and well-being that often results from activities that require intense concentration and effort of the mind and body functioning as an integrated whole. Many have experienced this feeling, but few have been able to put it into words.

CHAPTER 2

Questions and Answers

WILL WEIGHT TRAINING MAKE ME MUSCLE BOUND?

No, weight training will not make you muscle bound if you follow correct weight training principles. Muscle bound refers to a condition in which a person has a limited range of joint motion. Correct weight training principles include training each muscle through a full range of motion. Each muscle is required to exercise from full extension to full contraction. Also, the opposing muscles receive an equal amount of exercise so that the muscles on one side of the joint do not overpower those on the other side. When these principles are followed, the weight trainer generally experiences an increase in joint mobility rather than a decrease. There are many more fat bound people than there are muscle bound.

Athletes frequently become muscle bound because of the unbalanced muscular development of most sports. Also, when athletes train with weights to improve their sports performance, they generally train only those muscles that are already overdeveloped and ignore balanced development. The result is that the athlete will often see weight training as the reason for their muscle bound condition when in fact their condition is the result of a poorly planned training program.

The gymnast is probably one of the best examples of a high level of strength development accompanied by a high level of flexibility. Strength and flexibility are compatible if correct training principles are followed.

WHEN I STOP WEIGHT TRAINING, WILL MY MUSCLES TURN TO FAT?

No, it is physiologically impossible for muscle tissue to become fat tissue. When you stop training the muscular system, the muscles will adapt to the new demand. If the new demand is low, the muscles will respond by getting smaller and weaker (atrophy). If caloric consumption is maintained at the level that was necessary for long periods of daily physical activity, the extra calories will now be stored as fat. This process used to be most obvious in the football player. During the season, this athlete would participate in three to four hours of physical activity including heavy weight training workouts to gain muscle mass for size and strength. During that time, he might be consuming ten thousand calories per day. After the last game, there were no more football practices, and his physical activity level dropped immediately to sedentary. Did the football player change his eating habits immediately? Usually not, therefore the muscle atrophied and fat accumulated, resulting in the myth that the muscle had turned to fat.

WILL WEIGHT TRAINING SLOW MY SPEED?

Muscle contraction is responsible for all human movement. Generally, a stronger muscle can move a body part faster. The research on this topic indicates that weight training increases speed. Muscular weakness and excessive body fat will slow your speed.

WILL WEIGHT TRAINING RUIN MY COORDINATION?

There is some adjustment to an increase in strength; however, most people can make this minor adjustment with no problem since strength gain is relatively slow. For the athlete engaged in a sport where "touch" is critical, it is probably best to increase strength during the off season and maintain that strength level through the competitive season. For the untrained individual, weight training may improve coordination.

IS WEIGHT TRAINING BAD FOR MY HEART?

There is absolutely no foundation, evidence, or indication to support this idea. Weight training does not damage a normal, healthy heart.

COULD HEAVY WEIGHT TRAINING CAUSE A HERNIA?

It is possible, but not very likely. A hernia is usually the result of holding your breath and straining to lift an object that is too heavy. This most often happens to individuals who do not train on a regular basis and do not know their own capability or correct lifting technique. The unfit person moving furniture is a classic example. Correct weight training procedures require that you never hold your breath while lifting. Also, in weight training you should learn about and practice correct lifting technique. These two factors, along with knowing how much you can safely lift, reduce your risk of experiencing a hernia.

WILL WEIGHT TRAINING STUNT MY GROWTH?

Weight training does not seem to have any effect on height. It does result in stronger bones, ligaments, and tendons. Short men and thin men may train with weights to develop a more "masculine" appearance. A man may appear more muscular because he is short or may train with weights because he is short, but it was not weight training that made him short.

WILL WEIGHT TRAINING INJURE MY JOINTS?

Weight training exercises performed in a smooth, continuous manner, as they should be, will increase joint strength. Weight training exercises performed improperly could damage your joints. Jerking, throwing, and dropping weights is usually incorrect lifting technique and may result in injury.

WILL WEIGHT TRAINING MAKE A WOMAN MASCULINE?

Hormones, not weight training, determine if a woman appears more or less masculine. Most women will in fact appear trimmer at the same body weight because muscle is more dense than fat. Women who train with weights can develop a healthy, shapely, trim female figure.

DOES WEIGHT TRAINING DEVELOP TOTAL PHYSICAL FITNESS?

Weight training can develop total physical fitness if you follow a carefully planned circuit weight training program. Total physical fitness involves the development of cardiovascular endurance, strength, muscular endurance, flexibility, and the control of your body fat level. Weight training programs can best develop strength and muscular endurance. There are more efficient ways to develop the other aspects of total physical fitness. Muscle looks good on men and women. If you want to look good (physically fit), weight training is one of the most effective ways to bring about that change in appearance.

WILL WEIGHT TRAINING 'SHAPE UP' A CERTAIN PART OF MY BODY?

"Shape up" to many people means lose fat from a specific part of their body. This is referred to as spot reduction. Examples of this are sit ups to lose fat from the abdomen and hip extension to lose fat from the hips. Unfortunately, all of the information to date indicates that spot reduction does not work. Fat reduction requires total body fat reduction. This is best accomplished by reducing caloric intake (eating) and increasing caloric expenditure (exercise). The best type of exercise is one that uses the large muscles of the body in a rhythmic and continuous manner. A good example is walking. Exercises for a specific body part will firm up weak, sagging muscles and may result in a trimmer appearance but will not effectively reduce the excess fat deposited in that area.

CAN I GAIN ALL OF THE MUSCLE I NEED FROM SPORTS PARTICIPATION?

For the average person, sports participation is not of sufficient intensity, duration, or frequency to produce strength gains or even maintenance. Weight training can produce a strength gain stimulus in one minute that is greater than a muscle would receive in hours of participation in most recreational activities. Many recreational sports injuries are the result of placing an unfit body in a highly competitive situation. You need to gain strength to participate in sports, not participate in sports to gain strength.

DOES WEIGHT TRAINING REQUIRE LONG TRAINING SESSIONS?

Weight training is one of the most efficient forms of exercise. It is possible to train all of the major muscle groups in the body in fifteen minutes. This should be repeated two or three times each week. You won't find many exercise programs that are faster than that. The amount of time you need to spend training with weights will be directly related to the goals you set for yourself.

WHEN IS A PERSON TOO OLD TO START WEIGHT TRAINING?

A person is never too old to start a sensible weight training program. The training program is planned for the individual. Some people may be too unhealthy to start but never too old. Weight training can be beneficial for anyone who has a muscular system to maintain regardless of age. Your goals, training program, and results will be different, but weight training can be beneficial regardless of age, sex, race, or religion.

The list of questions about weight training is almost endless. The ones answered here represent some of the common fears of those who do not train with weights.

CHAPTER 3

Muscle Structure
and Function

GENERAL INFORMATION ABOUT YOUR MUSCULAR SYSTEM

There are approximately 600 muscles in your body that make up about 50 percent of your total body weight. Skeletal muscles account for about 40 percent of your total body weight, and the other 10 percent is primarily involuntary muscle of the circulatory and digestive systems. While muscles vary a great deal in size, shape, arrangement of fibers, and internal characteristics, they all perform the same general function—which is to provide movement. All human movement is the result of muscular contraction. Therefore, it is difficult to overemphasize the importance of muscle tissue and the muscular system.

CHARACTERISTICS OF MUSCLE TISSUE

EXTENSIBILITY. Extensibility refers to the ability of muscle tissue to be stretched. If muscle tissue could not stretch beyond its normal resting length, you would not have the mobility or range of motion that you now have.

ELASTICITY. Elasticity refers to the ability of muscle tissue to return to its normal resting length and shape after being stretched. If muscle tissue did not have elasticity, it would remain at whatever length you stretched it to.

EXCITABILITY. Excitability refers to the ability of muscle tissue to receive a stimulus from the nervous system.

CONTRACTILITY. Contractility is the quality that really sets muscle tissue apart. When a stimulus is received, muscle tissue can contract or shorten.

These four characteristics combine to make muscle tissue a very special kind of tissue. It is muscle tissue that is responsible for every movement your body makes.

TYPES OF MUSCLE TISSUE

CARDIAC. Cardiac muscle is found only in the heart and is considered involuntary muscle since it is not possible to consciously contract the heart muscle.

SMOOTH. Smooth muscle primarily lines internal structures such as blood vessels and the digestive tract. Smooth muscle is also considered involuntary, since its contraction and relaxation is generally an automatic function and not the result of conscious voluntary control.

SKELETAL. The primary focus of this book is the development of skeletal muscle which is attached to the bones or skeletal system. Skeletal muscle is voluntary muscle, and the contraction of skeletal muscle is a result of conscious voluntary control.

THE SKELETAL SYSTEM AS A LEVER SYSTEM

There are three classifications of levers: first class, second class, and third class. All three types of levers are found in the skeletal system of the human body. Not only are there three types of levers, but there are also six different kinds of joints which are considered freely movable. The result is a wide range of human movement possibilities. The movements that take place are the result of muscle tissue pulling on separate bones or tissues across a joint. Some joints such as the ball and socket joint of the shoulder have a wide range of movement possibilities that may be strengthened, whereas others such as the hinge joint of the elbow are limited to two movements, flexion and extension.

STRUCTURE OF SKELETAL MUSCLE

A complete muscle has connective tissue at each end which attaches muscle to bone. This connective tissue is called a tendon. The tendon is continuous with connective tissue that encloses the muscle tissue. Within the muscle are bundles of muscle fibers (cells). Skeletal muscle fibers (cells) are generally long and relatively small in diameter. Within each muscle fiber there are long threadlike structures called myofibrils. These myofibrils run lengthwise through the muscle fiber. Each myofibril consists of many sarcomeres attached end to end. The sarcomere is the basic contractile unit of skeletal muscle tissue. Within the sarcomere there are thin myofilaments (actin) and thicker myofilaments (myosin). According to the sliding filament theory of muscle contraction, the myosin filaments have cross bridges that contact the actin filaments. The actin and myosin filaments do not change in length, but the myosin cross bridges pull the actin filaments toward the center. Since the actin filaments are attached to the ends of the sarcomere as they are pulled toward the center, the sarcomere becomes shorter in length.

MUSCLE CONTRACTION AND EXERCISE MOVEMENTS

It is of critical importance to understand that muscle tissue can only contract or relax. Therefore, muscle can only pull on bones or stop pulling on the bones. Muscle tissue cannot push. There are exercises in which an object, such as a barbell, is pushed away from the body. This is accomplished by muscles pulling on bones which cause the joints to extend. There are also pulling exercises in which muscles pull on bones which pull a weight toward the body. All exercises involve muscles pulling on bones across a joint. Once again, muscle tissue can only pull on bones. The movement that takes place depends upon the structure of the joint and the muscle attachments involved.

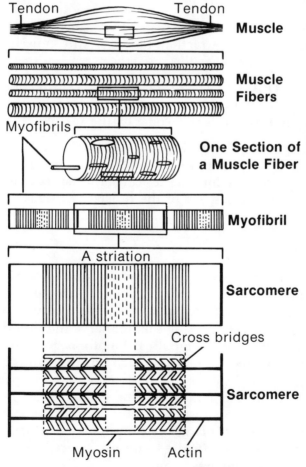

Redrawn from Jensen, Clayne R., Gordon W. Schultz, and Blauer L. Bangerter, *Applied Kinesiology and Biomechanics*, 3rd ed., McGraw-Hill Book Co., New York, 1983, p. 12.

ISOMETRIC CONTRACTION. Iso refers to equal and metric refers to length or measure; therefore, an isometric contraction is one in which the muscle maintains an equal length. This occurs when contracting a muscle and creating a force against an immovable object. The muscle contracts and tries to shorten but cannot overcome the resistance.

ISOTONIC CONTRACTION. Iso refers to equal or constant and tonic refers to tone or tension; therefore, an isotonic exercise is one in which movement occurs but muscle tension remains about the same. This includes most weight training exercise movements.

CONCENTRIC CONTRACTION. A concentric contraction is a shortening contraction in which the muscle becomes shorter and overcomes the resistance.

ECCENTRIC CONTRACTION. An eccentric contraction is a lengthening contraction in which the muscle contracts and tries to shorten but is overcome by the resistance.

ISOKINETIC CONTRACTION. Iso refers to equal or constant and kinetic refers to motion; therefore, a true isokinetic contraction is a constant speed contraction. Generally, it is the speed of the resistance that is controlled.

MOTOR UNIT

A motor nerve is a nerve that comes from the brain or spinal cord and causes something to happen, as opposed to a sensory nerve that takes information to the central nervous system. A motor unit consists of a single motor nerve and all of the muscle fibers to which it sends impulses. A motor nerve is connected to many muscle fibers. However, each muscle fiber is controlled by only one motor nerve. A motor nerve that is responsible for very fine movement may only be connected to ten muscle fibers, such as those responsible for eye movements. A motor nerve responsible for large or heavy human movements may be connected to five hundred muscle fibers, such as those responsible for hip extension.

THE ALL OR NONE PRINCIPLE. A muscle fiber contracts completely or not at all. If a single stimulus for contraction is below the threshold value, no contraction occurs. If the stimulus is above the threshold value, complete contraction occurs. All of the muscle fibers in a motor unit contract completely or not at all.

RECRUITMENT. There are hundreds of motor units in each muscle. The force exerted by a muscle is determined by how many motor units are recruited for a task and how frequently stimuli are sent to each motor unit.

MUSCLE ATROPHY AND HYPERTROPHY

Muscles that are not used will shrink in size (atrophy) to that size which is adequate for the demands placed upon them. A good example of muscle atrophy occurs with a broken leg or arm that is immobilized in a cast during the healing process. When the cast is removed, that arm or leg is much smaller than the active limb. The same thing happens to people who do not train their muscular system; however, the reduction in size occurs in both limbs and is so gradual that it often goes unnoticed.

The opposite is also generally true, that is, muscles that are forced to work harder than normal generally hypertrophy or increase in size. This muscle growth is much more visible and more pronounced in men that it is in women. The reason for this greater increase in muscle size in men is thought to be related to the hormone testosterone.

As your curiosity about muscle structure and function increases, refer to current human anatomy, human physiology, and exercise physiology textbooks for detailed information.

CHAPTER 4

Warm Up, Flexibility, and Stretching

WARM UP

An adequate warm up for weight training can be effectively achieved by performing a warm up set or sets of each exercise before progressing to heavier developmental sets. For example, if your weight training program begins with squats, you could perform a light set of squats in a slow, smooth, stretching manner to stretch and warm up the exact muscles and joints that will be involved when you perform heavier sets of this same exercise to develop strength. Almost all olympic lifters, power lifters, and body builders warm up for heavy exercises in this manner. This method of warm up seems to be beneficial for the psychological preparation (mental) as well as the physiological preparation (physical) to exert maximal or near-maximal effort.

It can also be beneficial to perform some type of cardiovascular endurance activity such as running, walking, or bicycling to warm your body before training with weights.

FLEXIBILITY

Flexibility refers to the range of motion available in each joint. It is specific to each joint. Those who do not perform any exercise, those who only participate in one sport, and athletes who have trained with weights but have used partial movements or have neglected to develo the opposing muscle groups are frequently less flexible than those who train correctly with weights. Correct weight training, through a full range of motion, may increase your flexibility.

How much flexibility is enough? There is no set measurable standard, but generally a joint should move freely in all of the directions that are appropriate for that joint.

STRETCHING BEFORE WEIGHT TRAINING

Many people feel better if they stretch their muscles and joints before more vigorous exercise. This stretching may help prevent exercise injuries and may improve performance, though there is little conclusive research evidence to support either of these common beliefs. At any rate, stretching can maintain or increase flexibility and may be done for that reason alone. It may also help relieve some of the muscle soreness that accompanies the early stages of a weight training program.

FOUR-MINUTE STANDING STRETCH ROUTINE

This stretching routine was designed to stretch all of the major joints and muscles in the body in a systematic manner while in a standing position. This stretching routine eliminates the need for you to lie down and roll around on the wet, muddy, dirty ground or on a dirty weight room floor. It can be done almost anywhere at anytime, safely and effectively.

Each stretch position is a static or held position. You should stretch a muscle about 10 percent beyond normal to develop flexibility, but since that is difficult to determine, stretch to the point where you can feel tension in the muscle being stretched and there is a moderate amount of discomfort. CAUTION: Avoid extreme pain.In this case, more is not better. Moderate discomfort in the muscle has a develomental effect (flexibility), whereas extreme pain may result in injury. Once a muscle is stretched to the level of moderate discomfort, hold that position for ten to thirty seconds. You could repeat each exercise up to three times. If you do repeat each exercise, you will develop more flexibility, but of course it will take longer to complete your stretching exercises. These stretching exercises should be repeated at least three times each week; therefore, one of the best times to do them is just before your weight training exercises.

STRETCHING EXERCISES

Start in a standing position two or three feet in front of a wall.

(1)   **(2)**

NECK. While keeping your body in a straight standing position, (1) bend your neck so that your head is face down and forward as far as it will go; (2) bend your neck so that your head is tilted as far as possible to the right; (3) bend your neck so that your head is back as far as it will go and your face is up toward the ceiling; (4) tilt your head to the left as far as possible. The stretch should be felt in the muscles of the neck. These are four separate static hold positions, not head or neck rolls.

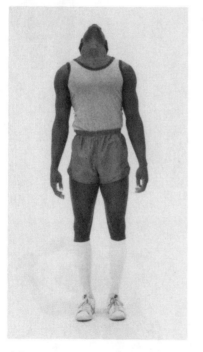

(3)

(4)

TRUNK. To stretch the spine and the major muscles of the torso: (5) bend forward at the waist and let your upper body hang forward and down. Keep your back rounded and your knees straight. Just hang there and let gravity pull on your upper body. (6) Stand up straight, then bend directly to the

(5)   (6)

(7)   (8)

right side. Pull your top arm across and behind your head so that the stretch is felt all the way along the left side of your body. (7) Bend backward with your arms extended overhead to stretch the muscles on the front of your body. (8) Bend to the left side, pulling the right arm across and behind your head so that the stretch is felt all along the right side of your body.

TRUNK TWIST. (9) Stand about two feet from a wall, facing away from the wall with your feet shoulder width apart and pointing straight ahead. Try to keep your feet in that position while you twist your body so that both hands may be placed on the wall at shoulder level. As much as possible, your head and shoulders should be facing the wall, while your feet and legs face away from the wall. (10) Return to the starting position and twist the opposite direction.

(9)

(10)

SHOULDERS. (11) From a straight standing position, join your hands together behind your back, interlocking your fingers. Keep your elbows straight while you raise both arms as high as possible behind your back toward the level of your shoulders. (12) Stand facing the wall about two arm lengths away from the wall. Lean forward and place both hands on the wall about head high and shoulder width apart. Bend forward at the waist, placing the shoulder joint on a stretch.

(11)   (12)

ELBOWS, WRISTS, AND FINGERS. (13) Stand facing the wall about one and one-half arm lengths from the wall. Place the palms of your hands on the wall with your fingers pointing down, your elbows straight and your hands about shoulder height and width. (14) Remain in the same position as the previous exercise, but place the back of your hands on the wall with your fingers pointing down. During both of these stretching exercises, keep the palm or back of your hands flat on the wall while placing them as high as possible.

(13)   **(14)**

HIP. (15) Spread your feet to the side by about three times the width of your shoulders. Bend the knee of the right leg and lean the upper body to the left side directly over the straight leg, placing the muscles on the inside of the left leg on a stretch. (16) Bend the knee of the left leg and lean the upper body to the right side directly over the straight leg, placing the muscles on the inside of the right leg on a stretch. (17) With your feet about shoulder width apart, assume a full squat position with your chest against your thighs. (18) Raise your hips from the full squat position, put your feet together, and wrap both arms around your thighs, keeping your chest against your thighs. You will probably need to keep your knees slightly bent.

(15)   (16)

(17)   (18)

HIP AND KNEE. (19) From a standing position with your feet together, keep your back flat and your knees straight while you bend forward at the waist. This stretch should be felt in the hamstring muscles on the back of your thigh.

(19)

HIP, KNEE, AND ANKLE. (20) From a standing position with your left side toward the wall, place your left hand on the wall for balance. Bend your right knee, raising your right foot toward the rear. Using your right hand, grasp your right foot on or near the toes and pull the foot so that the leg is placed in full knee flexion with the lower leg against the back of the thigh. Keep your knee pointing straight down. (21) Turn your right side toward the wall and repeat the previous exercise using the left leg.

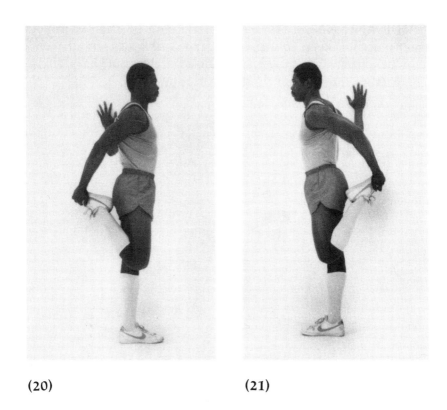

(20)   (21)

ANKLE. (22) Stand facing the wall about two arm lengths away. Step forward with your right foot and place both hands on the wall. Keep your left foot flat on the floor and pointing straight forward. The stretch should be felt on the back of the lower left leg. (23) Change legs and stretch the right ankle and lower right leg.

(22)   (23)

This brief standing stretch routine would be good alone or
before almost any physical activity. It is recommended here as a
means of maintaining or increasing your flexibility and
warming up for your weight training exercises.

CHAPTER 5

Guidelines for Performing A Weight Training Exercise

Follow these general guidelines for performing a weight training exercise to maximize your weight training progress and for safety.

STRICT EXERCISE FORM. By maintaining strict exercise form, you will keep the load on the muscles that you are trying to develop. When you find ways to cheat on an exercise, you will reduce the load on the muscles you are trying to develop and increase your risk of injury.

SMOOTH MOVEMENT. Weight training exercises should be performed in a smooth, continuous movement. Some exercises are performed faster than others and some involve acceleration, but they should all be smooth. This allows the muscle to apply force to the resistance throughout the full range of motion. The purpose of weight training is to build healthy muscle tissue, not to tear it apart.

FULL RANGE OF MOTION. Whenever possible, a muscle should be exercised from full extension to full contraction and back to full extension. This results in strength gains throughout the complete range of motion of the muscle in the concentric phase (shortening) and the eccentric phase (lengthening). It also helps prevent a loss of flexibility.

CONCENTRIC PHASE. The concentric phase of an exercise is the phase in which the muscle contraction overcomes the resistance. This results in the muscle getting shorter as the weight is raised. For most exercises, this concentric phase should take approximately one to two seconds.

ECCENTRIC PHASE. During the eccentric phase of an exercise, the same muscles that raised the weight now lower the weight. The resistance or weight is allowed to overcome the muscle contraction. Therefore, even though the muscle is contracting and trying to shorten, it is being lengthened by the pull of the resistance. Eccentric contractions allow us to lower a weight smoothly and a weight should almost always be lowered in a smooth, continuous manner. The eccentric phase of an exercise should take at least as long as the concentric phase (one to two seconds) and perhaps up to twice as long (two to four seconds) in some exercises. The same muscles are working to raise and lower the weight. Do not perform half an exercise by allowing the weight to drop.

Among those who gain the least from an exercise are those who throw the weight upward using poor exercise form, incorrect muscle groups, and momentum to raise the weight. Then, once the weight has been raised, they let it drop. Those individuals may move more weight, but they receive less benefit from the exercise and have a much greater risk of injury.

BREATHING. A good general rule for breathing during weight training exercises is to exhale during the greatest exertion, generally the concentric phase of the exercise, and inhale during the eccentric phase. One exception to this rule occurs when performing overhead pressing movements. It is more comfortable to inhale as the weight is pressed overhead and exhale as it is lowered. Breathing is an important part of correct exercise technique and needs to be practiced as the exercises are being learned with lighter weights. A definite breathing pattern should be learned for each exercise. There is some room for individual differences. However, the one thing that should be avoided at all times is holding your breath and straining to move a weight. This produces a great deal of pressure inside the chest and abdominal cavities and may result in dizziness, blackout, stroke, or hernia.

CONCENTRATION. Focus your full attention on the muscle as it moves the weight. This concentration should be maintained on every repetition and throughout every set to gain the maximum benefit from the exercise. Remember that the same muscle is working all of the time during an exercise, the concentric phase (raising the weight) and the eccentric phase (lowering the weight).

ISOLATED INTENSITY. Isolated intensity is closely related to concentration and getting the most out of your weight training in the least amount of time. Isolate a muscle or group of muscles that you wish to develop and force them to work very hard. As you advance in your muscle training, you will need to learn how to force a muscle to work to temporary failure—not

the point where you would like to quit, but the point at which the muscle cannot perform the task. This is very intense exercise for an isolated muscle and is much more effective in producing gains than easier sets that are stopped when they begin to get hard.

CHAPTER 6

Beginning Weight Training Programs

Two training programs for beginners will be presented in this chapter. One program will be for the "Universal" or weight stack type of equipment. The other program will be for barbells. These have been selected because they represent the weight training equipment that is most commonly available to beginners. Weight stack equipment has the advantages of safety, speed of changing weights, and ease of learning the exercises. The barbell has the advantages of variety of exercise movements, lower cost, greater mobility,and fit. Barbells fit everyone—body size is not a factor as it is on some exercise machines.

MEDICAL CLEARANCE

A complete physical examination is a good idea before starting any exercise program. Tell your physician that you want to start a weight training program and ask if there is any reason why you should not. This medical clearance becomes increasingly important as you get older, if you are overweight, and if you have not participated in a physical training program for a long period of time.

CLOTHING

For weight training, your clothing shold be loose enough to allow complete freedom of movement during all exercises. Exercise clothes should not be tight or restrict a complete range of motion. Most weight trainers choose to wear gym shorts, a t-shirt or tank top, socks and shoes when the training environment is warm. When the training environment is cold, a sweatsuit is usually worn over the shorts and shirt. Cotton material absorbs perspiration better than most synthetic materials and tends to be more comfortable during exercise.

TRAINING PARTNER

A good training partner can be your greatest asset. A bad training partner can be your greatest liability. A good training partner makes training safer by being ready to spot on hazardous exercises so you can train to the limit of your muscles' capability without fear of injury. A bad training partner is never ready when you need a spotter or is not paying attention during your exercises. A good training partner is always ready to help you load weights, change weights, and move equipment. A bad training partner lets you do all of the work of setting up for exercises. A good training partner offers positive motivation and encouragement. A bad training partner maintains a negative attitude which dampens your enthusiasm. A good training partner is on time for every training session. A bad training partner frequently skips workouts or arrives late.

You can make your best weight training progress with a good training partner. You can also make excellent progress training alone. If you have a bad training partner, talk with him or her about those qualities which they have that are hindering your weight training progress. If they are unwilling or unable to change, train alone or find a new training partner. By the way, be prepared to listen. You may have an opportunity to hear about some of your own faults as a training partner.

BASIC BARBELL GRIPS AND LIFTS

BASIC BARBELL GRIPS. There are three basic grips used in training with barbells: the pronated grip, the supinated grip, and the mixed grip. The pronated grip (thumbs in) is also referred to as the overhand grip, overgrip, or regular grip. The supinated grip (thumbs out) is also referred to as the underhand grip, the undergrip, or the reverse grip. The mixed grip has one hand turned each way.

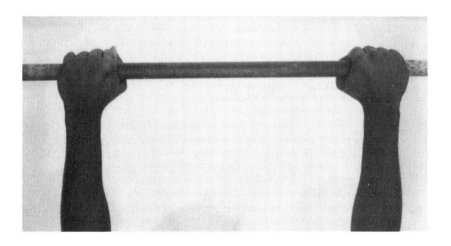

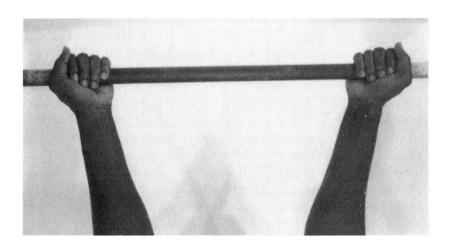

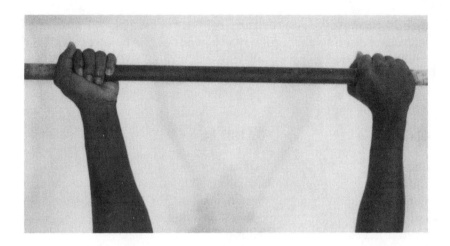

DEAD LIFT. When you are training with barbells and dumbbells, they must often be lifted from the floor to assume the exercise position. This should always be done with your knees bent, back flat, head up, and hips low. The leg muscles should be used to stand up from this squatting position. There is an exercise that involves this movement, and it is called the dead lift.

CLEAN. A clean is like a fast dead lift in which the weight is accelerated upward from the floor. The momentum is allowed to carry the weight upward as the arms are rotated under the bar and it finally comes to rest at the shoulders. This movement is often used when a barbell exercise starts at shoulder level, such as the military press.

EXERCISES

All of the exercises suggested for the beginning programs are described in the exercise sections of this book. One exercise for each major muscle group is all that is needed for the beginning weight trainer. In fact, for the first year or two of training, one exercise per body part will usually produce the best results. For those interested in physical fitness, there is usually no need to ever go beyond one exercise per body part. More is not always better.

UNIVERSAL	**BARBELL**
Leg Press	Squat
Calf Press	Calf Raise
Bench Press	Bench Press
Lat Pull	Barbell Rowing
Seated Press	Military Press
Pulley Curl	Barbell Curl
Curl Ups	Curl Ups
Back Extension	Straight Leg Dead Lift

FREQUENCY

Perform these exercises three times each week with at least forty-eight hours rest between training sessions.

SETS, REPETITIONS, AND RESISTANCE

START LIGHT AND PROGRESS SLOWLY. When starting a weight training program it is important to start with light weight and progress gradually as your body adapts to the new demands that are being placed upon it. Weight training is one of the most intense forms of exercise available. It is possible to isolate a muscle or group of muscles and work them to the point of failure within one or two minutes without experiencing total body fatigue. There are few other training methods that allow you to do that. Therefore, the tendency is for the beginner to want to overtrain. This tendency is also a product of the attitude that "if a little is good, more must be better." This is not always the case with physical training. With weight training it is very easy for the beginner to overtrain the muscles to the point that they cannot recover before the next training session. The end result is a decrease in performance or no gain. The programs suggested in this chapter are for healthy young adults of high school or college age (fifteen to twenty-two years old) who are near their peak of physical growth and who have been physically active. If you are older or have been inactive for a long time, progress more slowly.

THE FIRST FEW WEEKS. What is most important during the first few weeks of a weight training program? Use light weights and learn correct exercise technique. Learn the breathing pattern that works best and develop the habit of breathing during your exercises so that later, as the weight becomes heavier, you will not be tempted to hold your breath as you attempt to lift a difficult weight. Allow your body to gradually adapt to this new demand. Progress slowly to keep muscle soreness to a minumum. Gradually learn to increase concentration and intensity.

WEEKS ONE AND TWO (1 x 20) For the first two weeks, perform each exercise once (1 set), completing twenty exercise movements (20 repetitions) each set (1 x 20). Each time you complete twenty repetitions with a given weight, raise the weight for the next training session. Do not sacrifice proper exercise performance to complete the repetitions. When you can no longer perform the repetitions in strict exercise form during a set, it is time to end that set. If a weight feels very light and the sets are very easy, make a large increase in the weight for the next training session. If a weight feels moderately difficult, make a small increase for the next set. At the end of two weeks (six training sessions), you should be working at a weight with which it is difficult to complete twenty repetitions.

WEEKS THREE AND FOUR (1 x 20) (1 x 10). During the next two weeks (six training sessions), perform one set of twenty repetitions as a warm up set and one set of ten repetitions with a heavier weight. Each time you complete ten repetitions in the second set, raise the weight used in that set for the next training session. Following this procedure, you should be able to find the heaviest weight that you can lift ten times while maintaining strict exercise form.

WEEKS FIVE AND SIX (DeLorme) or (2 x 10). During weeks five and six, one option is to use the DeLorme method of progressive resistance. The first set of ten repetitions should be performed with 50 percent of your ten repetition maximum (10 RM). Your ten repetitions maximum is the heaviest weight that you can lift ten times. The second set of ten repetitions should be performed with 75 percent of your ten repetition maximum. The third set should be performed with 100 percent of your ten repetition maximum, or the heaviest weight that you can lift ten times. When you can complete ten repetitions in the third set, raise the weight used in that set for the next training session and adjust the first two sets according to this new 10 RM. You should be able to get about eight repetitions in the last set with the new weight. Keep working with that weight until you can get ten good repetitions, then raise the weight again. You should never get less than six good repetitions in the last set. If you cannot get at least six good repetitions, you have increased the weight too much and should reduce the weight for the next training session.

DeLORME METHOD.
1st set 10 reps with 50 percent of 10 RM
2nd set 10 reps with 75 percent of 10 RM
3rd set 10 reps with 100 percent of 10 RM

The DeLorme method is fast and easy on a weight stack machine but involves a great deal of weight changing when using a barbell, especially if you are alternating sets with a training partner. Therefore, another option during weeks five and six is to perform two sets of ten repetitions with about one or two minutes rest between sets. When you can complete ten repetitions in both sets, raise the weight used for that exercise during the next training session. You should be able to complete ten repetitions in the first set and six to ten repetitions in the second set.

Both of these options work well. Either may be used on Universal or with a barbell.

After six weeks, you should have had time to develop some basic strength and to finish reading this book so that you are able to develop your own training program based upon the goals you have set for yourself.

CHAPTER 7

Goal Setting

Goals are an extremely important part of any successful weight training program. It would be difficult to put the necessary effort into weight training if there was not some desirable goal to be reached. Not only does a goal give purpose to your training, but it is impossible to plan a weight training program without a goal. A training program is based upon the desired outcome. If you don't have a desired outcome, how can you plan for it?

A FORMULA FOR SUCCESS

What is success? This word has a different meaning for each of us. For the presentation of the formula, success will be defined as setting a goal and achieving it. Successful people achieve the goals they have set for themselves. A successful person reaches big success as a result of many smaller successes. Success breeds success. It is important to achieve smaller goals that lead to larger ones. This process should result in a life-style that is as enjoyable as the attainment of the goal.

GOALS. Be as specific as possible in defining your goal. This may be difficult if you are just beginning a new activity such as weight training, but try to be as specific as possible. An example of a long-term goal for a young man might be to bench press 250 pounds. For a young woman, a long-term goal might be to reduce her waist circumference to 24 inches. A short-term goal for this same young man might be to increase his bench press by 10 pounds in the next 3 months. A short-term goal for this young woman might be to reduce her waist measurement 1 inch in the next two months.

Once you decide upon a goal, write it down. This step is very important. It is like making a contract with yourself. Your thoughts or spoken words have a tendency to become modified with the passing of time. Your written goal will remain the same every time you read it. Once you have written your goal, you may begin to steer a course rather than drift aimlessly. It is important to know where you want to go before and during your entire journey.

You will find that having a defined written goal makes decision making easier. If you know exactly where you want to go, it is a matter of deciding, "Yes, this will take me the in the right direction," or "No, this will take me in the wrong direction."

To obtain great success or achievement, goals must take into consideration your unique individual qualities. Don't set yourself up for failure. For example, most men will never bench press 600 pounds, and most women will never weigh a healthy 90 pounds. Set goals that are challenging, but attainable, based upon where you are starting and what you believe is possible for you.

Humans are goal-striving beings that find happiness in striving for and attaining worthwhile goals. Boredom is usually a result of not having goals. Some say that weight training is boring or that life is boring. Those who say that must not be working toward worthwhile goals that they have set for themselves. If you know what you are trying to accomplish, weight training and life become exciting adventures. Not easy, but certainly not boring. When people stop striving for goals, they stop growing.

POSITIVE THINKING. Positive thinking is such an essential ingredient of success that some people have identified it as the only one. One reason for this is that the goal setting stage is primarily an internal process that others do not see. Positive thinking, by contrast, is obvious to everyone who comes in contact with the individual.

Your subconscious mind works on what you feed it. One sure

way to short-circuit your success is to set a goal and not believe you can make it. Fill your mind with positive thoughts, send out positive thoughts, and resist the negative thoughts of others. Positive people see the good side of bad situations and the bright side of every situation. Is the glass of water half full or half empty? Your answer to that simple question may reveal a lot about your attitude. Many people dwell upon what they don't have and can't do, while some focus upon what they do have and can do.

Do not strive for success without happiness—it would be an empty success even if you could achieve your goal. Truly successful people enjoy what they are doing. Most people are as happy as they decide to be. True happiness is based on your internal reaction to external events.

Imagination is a stronger force than willpower. Form a clear detailed image or picture of what you really want. Everything starts with an idea. You will become that which you think about. If you dwell on failure, you will fail. If you dwell on success, you will succeed. Positive thoughts create positive things.

Desire is the power behind human actions. Successful people have an all-consuming, burning desire to reach their goal.

Positive thinking includes belief. Belief is more than wishing—it is knowing that you can achieve your goal.

SUBCONSCIOUS MIND. Nobody knows much about the subconscious mind, but we do know that it is extremely powerful and that it can solve our problems. The subconscious mind works day and night to bring about that which you imagine or visualize. That is why it is so important to use positive thinking at all times. If you think failure, it will help you fail; if you think success, it will help you succeed.

Program your subconscious mind through repetition. Repetition can accomplish great tasks. Read your goal out loud at least twice each day, morning and night. Read your weight training goal before each training session so that you know why you are there and what you need to accomplish.

Humans have an opportunity to participate in their own creation. You can become what you want to become. You can be the person you want to be. To use your subconscious mind, use auto suggestion and repeat your desire or goal to yourself on a regular basis. Once the idea is deeply imbedded, the subconscious mind will go to work to help you achieve your goal. After the subconscious mind has been programmed, you need not concern yourself with how you will reach your goal—the way will appear. It is a good idea to always keep a note pad and pencil handy, for ideas and solutions will come to you. These ideas need to be written down immediately so you can expand on them later. Often, if they are not written down they are gone. You may remember that you had a great idea but not be able to remember what it was.

PLAN. Take time to plan. Everyone has the same amount of time each week, so why do some people accomplish more than others? You need to learn to manage yourself and use your time wisely. A lack of time indicates a lack of organization. Some people say they don't have time to exercise. What they should say is that exercise is less important to them than anything else they do.

Effectiveness is doing the right things. This requires a focus on result. In your weight training program, be sure you are doing the things that lead to the achievement of your goal. Do ot spend time on things that don't matter to you.

Efficiency is doing things right. It has a focus on methods. Once you are sure you are doing the right exercises to reach your goals, perform them as efficiently as possible.

Plan time to continue learning about weight training. The more you learn, the better you can plan to reach your goals.

Constantly evaluate your progress and plan again. Take time to plan how you will reach your goal and continue to evaluate your progress toward that goal.

DO IT. All of the previous steps are useless unless you take action. The world is controlled by people of action. You can never get anywhere unless you move. Decide what activities will lead to your goals, then act upon your decision. Learn to act and make things happen instead of merely reacting to things that happen to you.

It is important to realize that work and sacrifice are required to reach your goals. There is always a price to pay for anything that is worthwhile. Do not expect to get something for nothing. You must work at success. Once you have decided what must be done, you must discipline yourself to do it.

One of the most common reasons for failure is failure to take action. Procrastination has probably caused more failure than any other single factor. Now is the time to take action, not later, tomorrow, someday, or sometime. Start now. The clock is already running, and it cannot be stopped or reversed.

Once you get started, you must persist. It has been said that persistence is a familiar word but a rare quality. Many who take the first step fail because they do not continue working toward their goal. Stick with it, don't give up—never give up. If your goal is worthwhile, it is worth your best effort.

A FORMULA FOR SUCCESS

1. Define your goal or goals.

> Set short-term goals that you can achieve and that will lead you to your long-term goals.
> Fix in your mind exact measurable goals.
> Write your goals down.

2. Use positive thinking.

> Believe that you can reach your goals.
> Have faith in your ability to achieve your goals.

3. Use your subconscious mind.

> Read your goals out loud at least twice each day, morning and night.
> Read your weight training goals before each training session.

4. Plan.

> Take time to plan so that all of your efforts are directed toward your goals.

5. Take action.
> Start working toward your goal and don't stop
> until you reach it.
> Enjoy the journey as well as the arrival.

This formula for success will work for anything you want. It is presented in this book to help you reach your weight training goals.

WEIGHT TRAINING GOALS

There are some guidelines for setting weight training goals. The goals need to be believable, achievable, reasonable, and attainable. Don't set yourself up for failure. A goal to bench press one thousand pounds by the end of this year is not reasonable. A goal to lose twenty pounds of fat by the end of the week is not possible. Set goals that you can sincerely believe in. Once you reach a goal, you can always set a higher goal. Remember—success breeds success.

Goals must be compatible. Running the marathon in less than two hours and performing squats with eight hundred pounds are not compatible training goals.

Weight training goals must be specific and measurable, as well as have a specific time for their attainment.

Examples:

Poor goal: Increase my maximum bench press (no set amount, no time limit)

Good goal: Increase my maximum bench press by ten pounds by (specific day, month, and year).

Poor goal: Firm up my muscles (too general).

Good goal: Increase my strength by increasing my training weights by five pounds in each exercise by (specific day, month, and year).

If you have too many long-term goals, conflict of interest almost always interferes with your progress. Don't have too many goals. Focus on a few things that are most important to you. If, however, you have several short-term body measurement goals that are compatible and that lead to the same long-term goal of looking good, you will be all right. The goals you set must be your own, not someone else's. They must be your goals and something you want.

If you do not want to increase your muscular strength, muscular size, or muscular endurance; if you do not want to perform better, look better, or feel better; if you cannot think of any goal that weight training can help you achieve; you will probably perceive weight training to be difficult, time consuming, and boring.

CHAPTER 8

Record Keeping
and Progress

RECORD KEEPING

After setting your goals, it is important to keep track of each training session. Write down what you do during each workout as soon as you have done it. Weight training is not an exact science. There are some general guidelines that have evolved, but there are many variables that can be changed and every individual responds differently. This information will become valuable to you as you measure your progress. You will be able to look back through your records and compare your progress (results) with your training (input). This will help you find which exercises and training methods work best for you.

The important things to record are the name of each exercise, the order in which they were performed, the resistance used in each set, the repetitions completed in each set, the day of the week, the date, and perhaps a general comment about how you felt or anything that might have had an influence on your training that day, positive or negative—such as "felt tired, only two hours sleep."

Keeping track of your weight training sessions also helps to ensure the correct exercise stimulus since you have a written record of what you were able to do during the last training session. There is a challenge to do a little better than the last workout, one more repetition, or five more pounds.

EXERCISE LOG

Open Page Log (example)

Monday, August 15, 1998

Bench Press
(weight) 135 x (reps) 10
(weight) 155 x (reps) 8
(weight) 175 x (reps) 6

Form Log (example)

See Figure 8-1.

MEASURING STRENGTH. Strength is the ability of a muscle to exert force. If you are training with weights to gain strength, you can measure your progress by periodically testing your one repetition maximum (1-RM) using the exercises that you perform in your training program. Your one repetition maximum (1-RM) is the heaviest weight that you can lift one time while maintaining strict exercise technique. Of course you will be limited to the heaviest weight you can move through the weakest point in the range of motion. But you will still find out what is the heaviest weight you can move through the full range of motion of the exercise, and this is one measurement of your ability to exert force.

To perform 1-RM strength tests, start with a warm up set of 10 repetitions with 60 percent of your previous 1-RM. Then perform one repetition at 80 percent, 85 percent, 90 percent, and 95 percent of your previous 1-RM. After these progressively heavier sets, try for a new personal record based upon how the 95 percent load felt. If 95 percent felt easy, you may want to try 10 pounds more than your previous 1-RM, if you believe you can make it. If the 95 percent set was very hard, you may want to just try two and one half pounds or five pounds more than your previous 1-RM. Rest two minutes between each lift and three to five minutes before attempting

Name: _____

Figure 8-1
STRENGTH AND MUSCULAR ENDURANCE PROGRESS LOG

Day/Date	M 15 Aug 98														
Exercise	Wt	Rep	Wt	Rep	Wt	Rep	Wt	Rep	Wt	Rep	Wt	Rep	Wt	Rep	
B Press	135	10													
	155	8													
	175	6													

your new personal record.

The first time you try this to establish your initial 1-RM, start with a light weight and perform 10 repetitions. Add twenty, ten, or five pounds each lift and perform one repetition until you find the heaviest weight you can lift one time while maintaining strict exercise form and technique.

If you cheat on an exercise to move a heavier weight, you are lying to yourself about your strength. There is also a greater risk of injury when you begin to perform exercises improperly to move a greater weight than you can really handle.

Use spotters for the exercises in which you could get trapped under a heavy weight. Do not try to perform 1-RMs in all of your exercises—select one, two, or maybe three.

The beginning weight trainer could test 1-RMs every four weeks for the first six months to one year. After that, increases come more slowly, so testing once every six to twelve weeks might be often enough.

MEASURING MUSCULAR ENDURANCE. Muscular endurance is the ability of a muscle to exert force for a long time or for many repetitions. If you are training with weights to gain muscular endurance, you could measure your progress by performing as many repetitions as possible with a given weight. Select a weight that is 50 percent to 70 percent of your one repetition maximum. Perform as many continuous repetitions as possible without any pause or stop between repetitions and while maintaining strict exercise technique. Test your muscle endurance once every four weeks using the same weight to measure your muscular endurance and evaluate to the effectivenes of your training program.

MEASURING SIZE. One of the easiest ways to measure changes in size is to measure the circumference of various body parts with a cloth tape measure. While circumference measurements include many other kinds of tissue (bone, fat, blood vessels, skin, etc.), muscle and fat are the two tissues that change most rapidly. If you are training your muscles hard and eating properly, your gains should be due to increased muscle and your losses should be due to decreased fat deposits.

Have your training partner measure you. It would be ideal to use a Gulick tape measure if one is available. A Gulick tape has a spring tension device on the end so that all measurements may be made with the same tension on the tape. If a Gulick tape is not available and measurements are taken with a standard cloth tape measure, the tape should be placed around the circumference so that it is firm, but not so tight that the skin is indented. Measure to the nearest one-eighth of an inch or one-half centimeter.

The following is a list of measurements that are commonly taken and which are most subject to change through training. Take all of these measurements the first time you are measured. After that, you may choose to just measure the ones you are the most interested in. Beginning weight trainers may want to measure once every four weeks for the first six to twelve months. After the first year, changes come more slowly so you might want to take measurements once every two or three months.

There is no standard set of body circumference measurements. The ones suggested here are ones that are commonly used. Since these are used to measure your progress, muscle gain or fat loss, be sure that they are taken exactly the same each time and if possible with the same measuring tape. For some body parts, two measurements are described—relaxed and flexed. If you are trying to lose excess body fat, use the relaxed measurements. If you are trying to gain muscle size, use the flexed measurements when one is given, and use the relaxed measurements for the other body parts.

All of the following measurements should be taken in a straight standing position with your muscles relaxed, feet about six inches apart, and the measuring tape horizontal unless the directions for that body part specify something different.

NECK

Relaxed. Measure at the smallest horizontal circumference.

SHOULDERS

Relaxed. Measure completely around the body at the level of the greatest shoulder width.

CHEST

Relaxed. Measure at the largest circumference during relaxed breathing. Do NOT lift your chest or flex your muscles.

Flexed (Expanded). Measure at the largest circumference of the chest with the lungs filled, rib cage lifted, and muscles flexed.

WAIST

Relaxed. Measure at the smallest circumference, which is usually at or slightly above the navel. The abdominal muscles should be in their normal state of tonus for a relaxed standing position.

Flexed. Measure at the smallest circumference with the abdomen pulled in as far as possible.

HIPS

Relaxed. Measure at the largest horizontal circumference.

Flexed. Tighten the muscles in the hip region and measure at the largest horizontal circumference.

For all of the following arm and leg measurements, the tape should be held perpendicular to the limb segment being measured. Measure both arms and both legs.

THIGH

Relaxed. Measure the largest horizontal circumference. This is usually near the top of the thigh.

Flexed. Slightly bend the knee joint and contract all of the thigh muscles. Measure midway between the hip joint and knee joint.

CALF

Relaxed. Measure at the largest circumference.
Flexed. Contract the muscles on the back of the lower leg. Measure the largest circumference.

UPPER ARM

Relaxed. Arms hanging relaxed. Measure midway between the shoulder joint and elbow joint.
Flexed. Raise your arm to shoulder height and to the side of the body. Bend your elbow and flex all of the muscles of the upper arm. Measure at the largest circumference.

FOREARM

Relaxed. Arms hanging relaxed. Measure the largest circumference.
Flexed. Slightly bend the elbow and wrist so that as many forearm muscles as possible can be contracted. Measure at the largest circumference.

Remember that these measurements are to provide information about the effectiveness of your training program. Be sure that they are taken the same way every time.

MEASURING BODY WEIGHT. If your goal is to change your body weight, this can easily be measured on an accurate scale. It is best to use the same scale, at the same time of day, wearing no clothing or as little clothing as possible.

MEASURING BODY FAT. Have skinfold measurements taken at sites where you are most interested in losing excess body fat. There are some fairly standard measurement procedures for the different sites. It would be best to have these measurements taken by someone who is trained and experienced.

CHANGES IN APPEARANCE. Photographs of various poses or standing relaxed can be an excellent means of checking your progress toward looking better. Changes that take place in appearance are gradual and cannot be seen as they occur. Also, photographs are the only way to really see yourself. Obviously, the photograph needs to be taken while you are wearing as little clothing as possible, such as a swimsuit. As much as possible, use the same camera, location, position, distance, etc. for subsequent photographs.

When training to improve appearance, many men are interested in developing muscle size. However, muscle size should not be increased without regard to balance and symmetry. Some men have trained one body part until it does not look like it belongs on that body. This is seldom an attractive or appealing appearance.

PROGRESS EVALUATION

Don't try to check your progress too often. Physical changes take time. Let your weight training program have time to work. Beginners might be able to measure once a month and see progress, but more advanced weight trainers might only check once or twice a year.

GENETIC POTENTIAL

Each person has an upper limit on the strength or size they can gain. For the beginning weight trainer, gains are relatively easy and rapid. As progress continues and a person nears his/her genetic potential, the gains become difficult and slow. One of the most intriguing aspects of weight training is that there is no way to know when you have reached your maximum potential or, in fact, if anyone has ever reached his/her maximum potential. After years of weight training, bodybuilders and strength athletes continue to improve, though the rate of improvement becomes very slow.

PROBLEM SOLVING

When you are not making progress toward your goal for a long period of time, two or three months, it is problem-solving time. Consider everything you can think of that could be responsible for your lack of progress. Change the one thing that you think is the most likely cause of your lack of progress. Allow three or four weeks for the change to start making a difference. After a month if no progress occurs, try changing a different variable. Give it time to work. Changing more than one variable at a time may leave you with more questions than answers. Changing too often, less than four to six weeks, does not allow enough time to find out what works for you and what does not. Keep in mind that what works for you now will stop working when your body adapts to it.

Some of the factors to consider in solving your weight training problems (lack of progress):

Amount of resistance.
Number of repetitions.
Number of sets.
Rest between sets.
Number of exercises per body part.
Total number of exercises performed.
Order of exercises.
Frequency of training.
Concentration during exercise performance.
Intensity of training.
Regularity of training, hour and day.
Motivation level.
Nutrition.
Rest.

Other activities.
Mental stress.
Drugs.
Alcohol.
Tobacco.

CHAPTER 9

Guidelines for Planning A Weight Training Program

BASIC WEIGHT TRAINING PRINCIPLES

There are three basic principles behind all weight training progress.

SPECIFICITY. You must exercise the muscle that you want to develop. You must also train the muscle for what you want to develop—strength, muscle size, or muscle endurance.

OVERLOAD. The overload principle is the basis of all training programs. In weight training it means the muscle to be developed must be overloaded or forced to work harder than normal.

PROGRESSION. Once your muscles adjust to a given load, it is no longer an overload. The workload must be gradually increased as the muscle adapts to each new demand.

CONSIDERATIONS IN PLANNING YOUR WEIGHT TRAINING PROGRAM

YOUR GOALS. Planning a weight training program must begin with what you wish to accomplish. With weight training there are three basic aspects of muscle fitness that you can train for:

(1) strength
(2) muscle size
(3) muscle endurance

Any weight training program you choose will probably result in some increase in all three areas. However, there are some general guidelines that have emerged from research and experience that will help you focus on the development of the aspect you are most interested in.

Untrained beginners gain on almost any weight training program as long as progressive overload is applied.

WHICH EXERCISES. There are so many weight training exercises to choose from. Which ones are the best? The best weight training exercises are the compound exercises that require more than one joint or muscle to move the weight. With compound exercises like the squat and bench press, large amounts of muscle are exercised at the same time.

Exercises that require both arms or both legs to work together allow the use of more weight and maintain a balance of development in both limbs.

Some basic exercises have evolved that almost all weight trainers use. These exercises are included in the beginner or basic weight training program presented in this book.

Choose exercises for your training program with overall development in mind. It is best to develop the entire body as opposed to the unbalanced development that results from ignoring certain body parts or overdeveloping one or two body parts.

Keep balanced development in mind as you select your exercises. Develop both sides of the body equally. Always exercise the opposing muscle or muscle group. In the beginning, if you do not know the muscles, remember that for every exercise action or movement you perform, there should be an opposite action or movement in another exercise. For example, if you have an exercise that develops elbow flexion, there should also be an exercise that develops elbow extension.

Isolation exercises with dumbbells are primarily used by body builders in the final preparation for a contest.

NUMBER OF EXERCISES. One exercise per body part is best for the beginning weight trainer. In fact, one exercise per body part is enough for all but the most serious high-level strength athletes and body builders. For the first year or two of training, more than one exercise for each muscle group may result in overtraining and slow your progress. One exercise for each major muscle group or body part will result in about eight to twelve basic exercises in your training program.

ORDER OF EXERCISES. Exercise the largest muscles first and work your way down to the smallest muscles last. The largest muscles require the most energy and need the smaller muscles to assist. If the smaller muscles are already fatigued, it is difficult to handle enough weight to properly exercise the large muscles. For example, most back exercises require elbow flexion. If the elbow flexors have already been exercised, they will fail before the larger back muscles. The largest muscles are located on the torso and the muscles get smaller as you proceed outward on the arms and legs.

There is also a work-rest theory to the order of exercises. If a muscle is worked during an exercise, it is allowed to rest during the next exercise. If you are exercising the opposing muscle groups, it is good to work a muscle, then let it rest as you work on the opposing muscle. Sometimes this is referred to as a push-pull theory. This idea allows you to complete more work in less time.

Another consideration with the order of exercises is whether to perform a circuit or to perform the exercises in a traditional (non-circuit) manner. When a circuit is performed, each exercise in your training program is performed once in a specified order. Then each exercise may be performed again in that same order, and possibly again. The traditional way of lifting weights is to perform all of the sets of one exercise before moving to the next exercise.

RESISTANCE. How much weight to use depends upon what you want to develop. The general rule is that for strength you need to use a heavy weight and low repetitions. For muscle endurance, use a light weight and high repetitions. Muscle size is in between with moderate weight and repetitions. It is a good idea to perform warm up sets before the heavy weight of strength training.

Strength (90 to 100 percent of 1RM)
Muscle Size (70 to 80 percent of 1 RM)
Muscle Endurance (50 to 70 percent of 1 RM)

STARTING WEIGHT. Start with a weight that is light so that it is easy to perform the exercise correctly. Gradually increase the resistance. Don't be in too big of a hurry to load up on exercises. Give your body time to adapt. You will experience better progress, less muscle soreness, and less frustration. There is plenty of time to add weight.

REPETITIONS. The resistance you choose will affect the repetitions that you perform.

Strength (1-5 repetitions)
Muscle Size (8-12 repetitions)
Muscle Endurance (20-50 repetitions)

Most experienced weight trainers perform moderate to high repetitions when they exercise the abdominals, lower back, forearms, and calves.

SETS. The resistance and repetitions influence the number of sets you will be able to perform for each exercise.

Strength (4-8 sets)
Muscle Size (3-6 sets)
Muscle Endurance (2-4 sets)

REST BETWEEN SETS. The amount of rest between sets is determined by what you are trying to develop.

Strength (2-4 minutes)
Muscle Size (1-2 minutes)
Muscle Endurance (45-90 seconds)

FREQUENCY. A muscle usually needs two or three days rest to recover and adapt before it is exercised again. Exercising a muscle 3 days per week with 48 to 72 hours rest between training sessions works very well for most weight trainers. Advanced weight trainers perform different exercises on different days so that they may exercise four, five, or six days per week, but not the same body parts or exercises each day.

FIXED OR VARIABLE EXERCISE LOAD. There are two basic ways a load is applied to each exercise—fixed or variable. With a fixed load, the resistance, repetitions, sets, and rest interval remain the same (fixed) during a training session for an exercise.

Example:
  Bench Press
  150 pounds
  10 repetitions
  3 sets
  1 minute rest between sets

With a variable method of loading, the resistance, repetitions, and rest interval may vary for each set of an exercise.

Example:
  Bench Press
  150 pounds: 10 repetitions
  170 pounds: 8 repetitions
  190 pounds: 6 repetitions
  210 pounds: 4 repetitions

PROGRESSION. Here are some general rules that may be helpful in applying the progression of the overload.

(1) Increase only one variable at a time.
(2) Increase reps or sets before increasing resistance.
(3) Decrease reps when you increase resistance or sets.
(4) Decrease the rest interval between sets to increase the workload for muscular endurance.

CHAPTER 10

Advanced Weight Training

Progressive overload is the basis of all weight training programs. There are many ways to overload the muscles. The overload that the muscles experience depends upon all of the following variables:

Which exercises are performed.
How many total exercises are performed.
How many exercises for each body part are performed.
The order in which the exercises are performed.
The amount of resistance or weight used in each set.
The number of repetitions per set.
The number of sets per exercise.
The amount of rest between sets.
The frequency of training sessions.
The method of progression.
Whether the exercise load is fixed or variable.
Whether the total body is exercised each training session or divided into a split routine.
The exercise intensity.

There seems to be an unlimited number of ways in which these variables may be changed and combined. Some of the more common training programs will be presented to give you an idea of the variety available to you in weight training. Keep in mind that all of these training programs are different ways to arrive at the same thing, progressive overload. The bottom line in any weight training program is a progressive overload which is appropriate for what you want to develop. If the overload is present along with adequate rest and nutrition, your body will usually adapt.

Beginning weight trainers seem to gain on almost any weight training program. The greatest danger for the beginner is overtraining. If you are training very hard and long but are not gaining and you feel tired all the time, you are probably overtraining.

Humans cannot maintain absolute peak condition for very long—probably a few weeks at best. Therefore, the highly trained advanced weight trainers, competitive lifters, and body builders use periodization or cycling. They divide the year into periods or cycles. Then they vary their training methods and intensity during the cycles so that they reach their peak condition during their competitive season and hopefully for their most important contest of the year.

INCREASING EXERCISE INTENSITY

One of the first things that weight trainers try to do as they advance in their training is to increase exercise intensity.

CONCENTRIC FAILURE. To reach concentric muscular failure, perform repetitions until you cannot perform another repetition while maintaining strict exercise form.

FORCED REPS. Forced reps are repetitions that are performed after concentric failure by having a spotter assist as little as possible to help you complete one or two more repetitions.

NEGATIVES. It is possible to lower a heavier weight than you can raise. Negatives are performed by having spotters assist in lifting the weight and allowing you to lower the weight. This is an advanced training method which results in a great deal of muscle soreness. It is not recommended for beginning weight trainers.

ECCENTRIC FAILURE. Eccentric failure involves the performance of negatives (lowering a weight) until you can no longer control the speed at which the weight is lowered. This is obviously very dangerous and is not recommended for beginners.

CHEATING. Cheating is the use of body movement to get past the weakest point in the range of motion of an exercise. This can be a useful means of adding to the overload for an advanced lifter; however, most weight trainers use cheating to make the exercise easier.

PRE-EXHAUSTION. Pre-exhaustion involves performing an isolation exercise for a muscle followed immediately by a compound exercise. The idea is to work the muscle to concentric failure with the isolation exercise, then to force the muscle to continue working with the assistance of other muscles that are not exhausted.

CYCLE OR PERIODIZATION. Advanced lifters use training cycles or periods in which they progressively increase exercise intensity to reach a peak during their competitive season. Beginning weight trainers do not need to use any of these methods of increasing exercise intensity as long as steady progress is occurring. Most of these techniques are only used for a short period of time by advanced weight trainers to overcome a plateau or period of no improvement.

TOTAL BODY AND SPLIT ROUTINES

TOTAL BODY TRAINING ROUTINES. Beginners and fitness weight trainers usually perform all of their weight training exercises at one time and repeat this procedure every other day. They exercise the total body in one training session.

SPLIT ROUTINES. As weight trainers advance and the total workload increases, many choose to split their exercises performing part of them one day and the rest of them on another day. One example is the four-day split in which half of the exercises are performed on Monday and Thursday and the other half are performed on Tuesday and Friday. An example of a four-day split is a push-pull routine in which the pushing exercises are performed on Monday and Thursday and the pulling exercises are performed on Tuesday and Friday. Most advanced body builders go to a six-day split as they get near competition. On a six-day split they perform about one third of their exercises on Monday and Thursday, one third on Tuesday and Friday, and one third on Wednesday and Saturday. The ultimate split is the blitz routine in which only one body part is exercised each day.

FIXED SYSTEMS

Fixed systems are those that do not change variables during a training session but may change a variable for the next training session.

SIMPLE PROGRESSIVE SYSTEM. A simple progressive system involves changing only one variable such as the resistance. One example would be performing one set of ten repetitions of an exercise. Since ten repetitions were completed, the weight would be increased for the next training session.

DOUBLE PROGRESSIVE SYSTEM. A double progressive system involves changing two variables such as resistance and repetitions. One example would be performing one set of twelve repetitions. Since twelve repetitions were completed, the weight would be increased for the next training session and the repetitions would be decreased to eight. The repetitions would then be increased by one each training session until one set of twelve repetitions is completed with the new weight. Then the weight would be increased and the repetitions decreased again. Continue in this manner, increasing the repetitions, then the weight.

ONE SET TO FAILURE. A variation of the double progressive system is one set to failure. In this system, one set of each exercise is performed to the point where you cannot perform another repetition maintaining correct exercise form.

A weight is used that causes this failure to occur between eight and twelve repetitions. When you complete twelve repetitions, raise the weight for the next training session.

SET SYSTEM. The set system involves performing more than one set of each exercise. In a fixed system, the repetitions remain the same for each set. One example is three sets of six repetitions. When you can perform six repetitions in all three sets, raise the weight for the next training session. This is a very good strength gain program for beginning weight trainers. It is particularly good if you are training with barbells because it reduces the amount of time you spend changing weights.

CIRCUIT SYSTEM. A series of exercises are performed in a sequence or circuit with one exercise at each station. You move from one exercise to the next performing one set of each exercise until each exercise in the circuit has been performed once. The entire circuit may then be repeated. A circuit is usually completed one to three times during a training session. Circuit training is often used by athletes or anytime there is a large group, limited time, and limited equipment. Circuit training allows a large number of people to get a good workout in a short time period.

AEROBIC CIRCUIT SYSTEM. In an aerobic weight training circuit, exercises are performed one right after the other with very little rest between exercises. This is done to keep the heart rate elevated during the entire circuit and thus produce a training effect for the cardiovascular system.

SUPER SET SYSTEM. A super set involves the performance of two exercises in a sequence, then a rest interval. Often opposing muscle groups are exercised in this manner. For example, the first set might be barbell curls for the elbow flexors. The next exercise could be tricep extensions for the elbow extensors. Since these muscles work in opposition to one another, one of them is resting while the other is working. After one set of each exercise, there is generally a rest interval before repeating the sequence. This is a good way to reduce your training time without reducing the amount of work completed during the training session. This is like a mini-circuit.

GIANT SETS. Giant sets usually involve three to five exercises for the same muscle. One set of each exercise is performed with little or no rest between sets. After each exercise in the sequence has been completed, there is a rest interval before the sequence is repeated. This is a very advanced training system that some body builders use. It is doubtful that a beginner could progress on such a system.

REST-PAUSE SYSTEM. There are many variations of this system. Here is one. Perform an exercise to the point of temporary muscular failure, hold the weight while the muscle recovers slightly, perform another repetition, pause, another repetition, and continue until no more repetitions can be performed.

VARIABLE SYSTEMS

Variable systems alter one or more variables during the performance of one exercise.

PYRAMID SYSTEM. In a pyramid system, the weight on each set of an exercise is increased with a corresponding decrease in the number of repetitions. This allows the exerciser to proceed from a light weight to a heavy weight. This system is most often used by those training for strength. Some choose to pyramid up only; others pyramid up to a heavy weight then back down again.

PERCENTAGE SYSTEM. This is usually a variation of the pyramid system in which the sets are performed at different percentages of the one repetition maximum for that exercise. The percentage usually starts low in the first set and increases in each of the following sets.

DELORME SYSTEM. One percentage system that is very

good for beginners and those training for fitness is the DeLorme system.

1st Set, 10 Reps, 50 percent of 10 RM
2nd Set, 10 Reps, 75 percent of 10 RM
3rd Set, 10 Reps, 100 percent of 10 RM

CONTINUOUS SET SYSTEM. In the continuous set system, start with a weight that can be used to complete a given number of repetitions, say ten repetitions. When you reach the point at which no more repetitions can be performed, have training partners remove a small amount of weight. Continue the exercise until no more repetitions can be performed. Again the training partners remove a small amount of weight. Continue this process until no more repetitions can be performed even with the lightest weight.

LIGHT TO HEAVY SYSTEM. This is a variation of the pyramid and continuous set systems. Start with a light to moderate weight and perform three repetitions. Have your training partners quickly add a small amount of weight. Perform three more repetitions and again add weight. Continue this process until only one repetition can be performed.

TONNAGE SYSTEM. The resistance and repetitions vary, but the lifter keeps track of the total pounds lifted in a training session. This is most often used by competitive weight lifters.

These are only a few of the ideas that advanced weight trainers have tried to improve their training progress. There are many, many more.

TRAINING EQUIPMENT

FIXED RESISTANCE EQUIPMENT. Barbells, dumbbells, and some weight stack equipment have a resistance that is a fixed weight that remains the same throughout the exercise.

Because of changes in leverage in the skeletal system during movement through the range of motion, this weight will be very difficult to move at some joint angles and very easy at other joint angles.

VARIABLE RESISTANCE EQUIPMENT. Some weight stack equipment is designed so that as changes in leverage in the skeletal system take place for the working muscle, compensating leverage changes take place in the machine. The weight in the stack lifted remains constant, but the leverage change in the machine makes the resistance greater at some angles and less at other joint angles. The idea is to keep the muscle working at its maximum throughout the full range of motion.

CONSTANT SPEED EQUIPMENT. There are several constant speed exercise devices which use different means to regulate the speed. The idea is accommodating resistance. The muscle can contract as completely as possible throughout the range of motion without creating a momentum problem.

No equipment has been proven superior. The muscles don't know or care what type of equipment is used as long as they are overloaded.

CHAPTER 11

Barbell and Dumbbell Exercises

There are many barbell and dumbbell exercises and several variations of each exercise. This chapter includes some of the more common exercises for you to try. As you progress in your weight training and plan new exercise programs, try new exercises. This will add new interest and excitement to your training.

This chapter is arranged in the following order.

Chest
    Bench Press
    Incline Bench Press
    Straight Arm Pullover
    Bent Arm Pullover
    Cross Bench Pullover
    Bent Arm Flyes

Back (Upper Back)
    Shoulder Shrug
    Power Cleans

Back (Lower Back)
    Dead Lift
    Straight Leg Dead Lift
    Good Morning Exercise

Back (Middle Outer Portion)
Barbell Rowing
Chin Ups
Pull Ups
Pull Ups Behind the Neck
One Dumbbell Rowing

Shoulders
Military Press
Press Behind the Neck
Upright Rowing
Lateral Raise
Bent Over Lateral Raise
Front Raise

Arm (Elbow Flexors)
Barbell Curl
Reverse Curl
Incline Dumbbell Curl
Seated Dumbbell Curl

Arm (Elbow Extensors)
Close Grip Bench Press
Lying Tricep Extension
Standing Tricep Extension

Arm (Forearm)
Barbell Wrist Curl
Reverse Wrist Curl

Leg (Upper Leg)
Squat
Front Squat
Lunge

Leg (Lower Leg)
Standing Barbell Calf Raise
One Dumbbell Calk Raise
Donkey Calf Raise

CONCENTRIC AND ECCENTRIC PHASE

CONCENTRIC PHASE. The concentric phase of a weight training exercise is that portion of the exercise during which your muscular contractions overcome the resistance and the weight is raised.

ECCENTRIC PHASE. The eccentric phase of a weight training exercise is that portion of the exercise during which the resistance overcomes your muscular contraction and the weight is lowered.

It is very important to remember that the same muscles are working during both the concentric and eccentric phases of a weight training exercise. Don't perform half an exercise; control the weight with your muscles throughout the exercise.

DUMBBELLS

Almost any barbell exercise can also be performed using dumbbells. Dumbbells are often used for isolation exercises by advanced body builders. In many dumbbell exercises, the dumbbells may be moved together or in an alternating manner.

CHEST

BENCH PRESS

Muscles developed: Pectoralis major, anterior deltoid, triceps.

Starting Position: Start in a position lying on your back on a flat bench holding a barbell directly above your shoulders. Your arms should be straight, and both feet should be flat on the floor.

Eccentric Phase: Inhale as you lower the bar to touch your chest.

Concentric Phase: Exhale as you press the weight back up to the starting position.

Spotting: You should have a spotter standing at the head end of the bench when you perform this exercise just in case you get stuck with the weight on your chest.

Variations: There are many variations of this basic chest exercise that result from changes in the angle of the bench and changes in the width of the hand spacing on the bar.

Additional Information: This exercise is easier to perform if you have a rack to hold the weight above the bench.

INCLINE BENCH PRESS

Muscles Developed: Upper pectoralis major, anterior deltoid, triceps.

Starting Position: Start in a position lying on your back on an incline bench holding a barbell directly above the shoulders. Both arms should be straight, and both feet should be flat on the floor.

Eccentric Phase: Inhale as you lower the bar to touch your chest.

Concentric Phase: Exhale as you press the weight back up to the starting position.

Spotting: You should have a spotter standing behind the bench in case you cannot get the weight back to the starting position.

Variations: Variations of this exercise result from changing the angle of the incline bench and from changing your hand spacing on the bar.

Additional Information: This exercise is much easier to perform if you have a weight rack to support the weight above the bench.

STRAIGHT ARM PULLOVER

Muscles Developed: This is primarily an exercise to lift and expand the rib cage.

Starting Position: Start in a position lying on your back on a flat bench holding a barbell directly above your shoulders. Your hand spacing should be about shoulder width.

Eccentric Phase: Inhale deeply as you lower the bar overhead, keeping your arms straight. When you reach the end of this

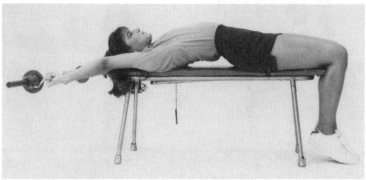

motion, hold this fully stretched position for three to five seconds with as much air in the lungs as they will hold.

Concentric Phase: Exhale as you return the bar to the starting position.

Additional Information: This is primarily a stretching exercise to lift and expand the rib cage. Do not attempt to handle heavy weight in this exercise.

BENT ARM PULLOVER

Muscles Developed: Latissimus dorsi, pectoralis major.

Starting Position: Start in a position lying on your back on a flat bench holding a barbell supported on your chest. Your hands should be six to twelve inches apart, your elbows bent, and your head hanging beyond the end of the bench.

Eccentric Phase: Inhale as you lower the weight past your face toward the floor.

Concentric Phase: Exhale as you pull the weight from the floor to the starting position.

Additional Information: Keep your elbows bent and your arms in close to your head.

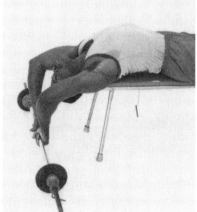

CROSS BENCH PULLOVER

Muscles Developed: This is primarily a stretching exercise to lift and expand the rib cage.

Starting Position: Start in a position lying across an exercise bench with your shoulders on the bench. Hold a dumbbell with both hands directly above your shoulders, keeping your arms straight.

Eccentric Phase: Inhale as deeply as you can while lowering the weight overhead. Keep your arms straight. Hold the fully

stretched position three to five seconds while maintaining as much air in your lungs as possible.

Concentric Phase: Exhale as you return to the starting position.

Additional Information: This is primarily a stretching exercise to lift and expand the rib cage. Do not attempt to use heavy weight in this exercise.

BENT ARM FLYES

Muscles Developed: Pectoralis major.

Starting Position: Start in a position lying on your back on a flat exercise bench. Hold one dumbbell in each hand above the shoulders with the arms slightly bent.

Eccentric Phase: Inhale as you move the dumbbells away from each other and lower them toward the floor.

Concentric Phase: Exhale as you return the dumbbells to the starting position.

Variations: This exercise may also be performed on an incline or decline bench.

Additional Information: Keeping your elbows slightly bent throughout this exercise will place the exercise stress on the pectoralis major muscle and relieve the stress on the elbow joint.

BACK (UPPER BACK)

SHOULDER SHRUG

Muscles Developed: Trapezius.

Starting Position: Start in a standing position with a barbell hanging at arms length in front of your body. Both hands should be holding the bar in a pronated grip (thumbs in).

Concentric Phase: Inhale as you lift or shrug your shoulders to the highest possible position. Hold that position briefly.

Eccentric Phase: Exhale as you slowly lower the shoulders back to the starting position.

Variations: (1) Roll the shoulders forward and up then back and down. (2) Roll the shoulders back and up, the forward and down.

Additional Information: Do not bend your elbows or pull with your arm muscles. The hands and arms serve as hooks to hang the weight on during this exercise. Do not jerk the weight upward or let it drop back to the starting position.

POWER CLEANS

Muscles Developed: Trapezius, erector spinae, gluteus, quadriceps.

Starting Position: Bend over and grasp a barbell that is lying on the floor. Your hands should be approximately shoulder width apart and in a pronated grip (thumbs in). Bend your knees and hips so that your hips are at knee level. Your head should be up and your back flat.

Concentric Phase: Inhale as you lift the bar from the floor and accelerate the bar upward, gaining speed as it rises to the highest position you can pull it to. The pull should continue upward to the level of your chest or shoulders. As the bar nears its highest point, quickly rotate your arms under the bar and bend your knees, catching the bar on your shoulders. Straighten your legs to a standing position and exhale.

Eccentric Phase: Inhale and quickly rotate the arms from under the bar. Bend the arms, legs, and hips to decelerate the bar to a hang position, then slowly bend the knees and hips to lower the bar back to the floor. Exhale.

Variations: (1) Start with the weight up on blocks. (2) Start with the weight in a hang position.

Additional Information: Keep your back straight. Do not jerk the weight from the floor, but lift and accelerate the weight.

LOWER BACK

DEAD LIFT

Muscles Developed: Erector spinae, gluteus, quadriceps.

Starting Position: Bend over and assume a mixed grip on a barbell that is lying on the floor. Bend your knees and hips so

that your hips are approximately knee level. Keep your head up and back flat.

Concentric Phase: Inhale, keep your head up and back flat while straightening the hips and knees to arrive at a standing position. Exhale.

Eccentric Phase: Inhale, keep your head up and back flat as you slowly lower the weight back to the floor by bending your knees and hips. Exhale.

Additional Information: Extremely heavy weight can be handled in this exercise. Progress slowly and maintain correct lifting position. Progressing too quickly or using improper lifting technique may result in injury.

STRAIGHT LEG DEAD LIFT

Muscles Developed: Erector spinae.

Starting Position: Bend over and grasp a barbell that is lying on the floor. Use a pronated grip (thumbs in).

Concentric Phase: Inhale and straighten the body to a standing position. Lift the bar upward while keeping the arms and legs straight. The bar should remain close to your legs, and you should maintain a smooth, steady lifting motion.

Eccentric Phase: Exhale while lowering the bar back to the floor. Keep the arms and legs straight.

Additional Information: This can be an excellent developmental exercise for the erector muscles of the spine when it is done correctly. Do not attempt to use heavy weight and low repetitions or try a maximum lift. Do not use a jerky lifting motion. Progress very slowly and cautiously.

GOOD MORNING EXERCISE

Muscles Developed: Erector spinae.

Starting Position: Start in a standing position with a barbell resting on your shoulders behind your neck.

Eccentric Phase: Inhale, keep your back flat and bend forward. Keep your legs straight.

Concentric Phase: Exhale while returning to the starting position.

Additional Information: Caution should always be used when exercising the muscles of the spinal column. Do not attempt to use heavy weight for low repetitions in this exercise. Do not attempt a maximum lift. Do not use a jerky lifting motion.

BACK (MIDDLE OUTER BACK)

BARBELL ROWING

Muscles Developed: Latissimus dorsi, rear deltoid, trapezius.

Starting Position: Start in a bent over position with your knees bent and a bar hanging directly below your shoulders.

Concentric Phase: Inhale as the weight is pulled upward until the bar touches your chest. Pause briefly.

Eccentric Phase: Exhale as the weight is lowered to the starting position.

Variations: (1) This exercise is sometimes performed while standing on a bench or block to get more stretch in the starting position as the weight increases and larger plates are used. (2) Changing the distance between your hands results in several variations of this exercise. (3) The bar may be pulled to the shoulders, chest, or abdomen to vary this exercise. (4) This exercise may also be performed with dumbbells either bringing both up at the same time or alternately.

Additional Information: Keep your back as flat as possible throughout this exercise. Do not jerk or drop the weight. Keep the knees slightly bent to reduce the stress on the lower back.

Perform this exercise with caution and common sense. The lower back is in a potentially dangerous position. To make this exercise safer for the lower back it may be performed with your forehead supported on a solid object that is about waist high.

CHIN UPS

Muscles Developed: Latissimus dorsi, biceps.

Starting Position: Start in a position hanging from a chinning bar with a supinated grip (thumbs out).

Concentric Phase: Exhale as you pull yourself upward to a position with your chin above the bar.

Eccentric Phase: Inhale as you slowly lower yourself to the starting position.

Variations: Changes in grip spacing result in several good variations of this exercise.

Additional Information: Start each chin up from a full hang. Do not bounce, kick, or use a whipping motion of the body,

because that will reduce the effectiveness of the exercise. One of the best ways to add weight to this exercise is to hang a dumbbell from a wide strap that passes behind your lower back and place the dumbbell between your thighs to keep it from swinging.

PULL UPS

Muscles Developed: Latissimus dorsi, biceps.

Starting Position: Start in a position hanging from a bar with a pronated grip (thumbs in).

Concentric Phase: Exhale as you pull yourself upward to a position with your chin above the bar.

Eccentric Phase: Inhale as you slowly lower yourself to the starting position.

Variations: Changes in grip spacing result in several good variations of this exercise.

Additional Information: Start each pull up from a full hang. Pause with your chin above the bar and slowly lower yourself to the starting position. Add weight by placing a dumbbell between the thighs suspended by a wide strap around the lower back.

PULL UPS BEHIND THE NECK

Muscles Developed: Latissimus dorsi, biceps.

Starting Position: Start in a position hanging from a bar with a wide pronated grip (thumbs in).

Concentric Phase: Exhale as you pull yourself upward to a position where the upper back touches the bar.

Eccentric Phase: Inhale as you slowly lower yourself to the starting position.

Variations: With the same hand spacing, pull upward with

the bar passing in front of your face until your chest touches the bar.

Additional Information: Start from a fully stretched hang position. Pause briefly at the top. Lower slowly to the starting position. Add weight by placing a dumbbell between the thighs suspended by a wide strap around the lower back.

ONE DUMBBELL ROWING

Muscles Developed: Latissimus dorsi.

Starting Position: Start with one hand and one knee on an exercise bench. The foot of your other leg should be on the floor and your hand on that side of the body should be holding a dumbbell hanging at arms length below your shoulder.

Concentric Phase: Inhale as you pull the dumbbell upward until it touches your chest. Pause briefly.

 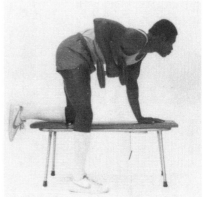

Eccentric Phase: Exhale as you slowly lower the dumbbell to the starting position.

Variations: Bring the dumbbell to the shoulder, chest, or waist to vary this exercise.

Additional Information: Use the hand and forearm as a hook to hold the weight while the back muscles pull the elbow to its highest position.

SHOULDER

MILITARY PRESS

Muscles Developed: Deltoid, triceps.

Starting Position: Start in a standing position with a barbell supported at shoulder level in front of the body. The hands should be slightly wider than shoulder width.

Concentric Phase: Inhale while pressing the weight overhead to a straight arm position.

Eccentric Phase: Exhale while lowering the weight to the starting position.

Variations: This exercise can also be done in a sitting position on a flat exercise bench or one that has a seat and near vertical back support.

Additional Information: This exercise is called the military press because you should stay in an erect posture (military posture) while forcing the muscles of the arms and shoulders to do all the work. Do NOT bend or sway the back to complete a repetition.

PRESS BEHIND THE NECK

Muscles Developed: Deltoid, triceps.

Starting Position: Start in a standing position with a barbell resting on the top of your upper back. Your hands are also supporting the bar and are wider than shoulder width.

Concentric Phase: Inhale as you press the bar upward to arms length overhead.

Eccentric Phase: Exhale as you slowly lower the bar to the starting position.

Variations: This is also an excellent exercise when it is performed in a sitting position.

Additional Information: Keep the back straight and make the arm and shoulder muscles move the weight. Do NOT lean back to complete a repetition.

UPRIGHT ROWING

Muscles Developed: Deltoid, trapezius.

Starting Position: Start in a standing position with a barbell hanging at arms length in front of the body. The hands should be in a pronated grip (thumbs in).

Concentric Phase: Inhale while pulling the elbows as high as possible in a smooth, continuous movement. The bar should reach chin level.

Eccentric Phase: Exhale while slowly lowering the bar to the starting position.

Additional Information: Concentrate on the deltoid muscles, raising the upper arm and keeping the elbows high. The arm muscles should be as inactive as possible.

LATERAL RAISE

Muscles Developed: Deltoid, trapezius.

Starting Position: Starting in a standing position with one dumbbell in each hand.

Concentric Phase: Inhale while moving the weights away from the body and upward. Keep the arms fairly straight and raise the weights to shoulder level.

Eccentric Phase: Exhale while lowering the weights to the starting position.

Variations: This exercise may also be done in a sitting position. The deltoid is a muscle with three fairly distinct portions: front, lateral, rear. The lateral raise tends to best develop the lateral portion. The front raise develops the front portion and the bent over lateral raise develops the rear portion.

BENT OVER LATERAL RAISE

Muscles Developed: Rear deltoid.

Starting Position: Start this exercise in a bent over position with the back flat and parallel to the floor. The knees should be slightly bent. One dumbbell is held in each hand, the arms are straight, and the dumbbell is hanging below the shoulder joint.

Concentric Phase: Inhale while raising the dumbbells to the side up to shoulder level. Pause briefly.

Eccentric Phase: Exhale while lowering the weights to the starting position.

Variations: This exercise may also be done while sitting on the end of a bench or while lying face down on a flat or incline bench that is high enough to allow the arms to hang fully extended.

Additional Information: Lift the arms straight to the side or move them slightly forward toward the head as the weight is lifted.

FRONT RAISE

Muscles Developed: Frontal deltoid, clavicular portion of pectoralis major.

Starting Position: Start in a standing position holding a barbell or two dumbbells hanging at arms length.

Concentric Phase: Inhale while raising the weight to shoulder level keeping the arms fairly straight. Pause briefly.

Eccentric Phase: Exhale while lowering the weight to the starting position.

Variations: This exercise may also be done to an overhead position as long as the back is not allowed to arch or bend.

On straight arm exercises a slight bend at the elbow may relieve unnecessary tension or strain in the elbow joint. This is not problem as long as it makes the exercise more productive for you. However, do not bend your elbows to make the exercise easier for the working muscles.

ARM (ELBOW FLEXORS)

BARBELL CURL

Muscles Developed: Biceps, brachialis.

Starting Position: Start in a standing position with a barbell hanging in front of the body. The hands should be gripping the bar at shoulder width with a supinated grip (thumbs out).

Concentric Phase: Exhale while raising the weight to the shoulders by moving only at the elbow joint.

Eccentric Phase: Inhale while lowering the weight to the starting position.

Variations: Any elbow flexion or curling exercise will develop the elbow flexor muscles. There are many variations of curling exercises. Variations of this standing curl may be achieved by changing the space between your hands when gripping the bar.

REVERSE CURL

Muscles Developed: Biceps, brachialis, brachioradialis, wrist and hand flexors.

Starting Position: Start in a standing position with a barbell hanging in front of the body. Both hands should be holding the bar in a pronated grip (thumbs in).

Concentric Phase: Exhale while raising the bar to the shoulders by bending only at the elbows.

Eccentric Phase: Inhale while lowering the bar to the starting position.

Variations: Changes in the distance between the hands will result in variations of this exercise.

Additional Information: This exercise provides a strong stimulus to the forearm muscles and is often used as a forearm exercise.

INCLINE DUMBBELL CURL

Muscles Developed: Biceps.

Starting Position: Start with your back against an incline bench. On some incline benches this will be a sitting position and on some incline benches it will be a standing position. Hold one dumbbell in each hand with the arms extended and hanging directly below the shoulder joint.

Concentric Phase: Exhale while bending the arms only at the elbows in pulling the weights to the shoulders.

Eccentric Phase: Inhale while lowering the weights to the starting position.

Variations: (1) Alternate arms so that one is coming up as the other is going down. (2) Turn the arms out so that the dumbbells are raised and lowered to the sides of the body instead of in front of the body.

SEATED DUMBBELL CURL

Muscles Developed: Biceps.

Starting Position: Start in a sitting position with one dumbbell in each hand.

Concentric Phase: Exhale while bending only at the elbows to bring the weights up to the shoulders.

Eccentric Phase: Inhale while lowering the weights to the starting position.

Variations: (1) Dumbbell curls may be performed standing, sitting, on an incline bench, or lying on your back on a flat bench. (2) There are a variety of arm positions that may be used when working with dumbbells. (3) Dumbbell curls may be alternated with one arm coming up while the other is going down.

ARM (ELBOW EXTENSORS)

CLOSE GRIP BENCH PRESS

Muscles Developed: Triceps, anterior deltoid, pectoralis major.

Starting Position: Start in a position lying on your back on a

flat bench holding a barbell directly above the shoulders with a close grip (6-8 inches) and the arms straight.

Eccentric Phase: Inhale as you lower the bar until it touches the chest.

Concentric Phase: Exhale as you press the weight back to the starting position.

LYING TRICEP EXTENSION

Muscles Developed: Triceps.

Starting Position: Start in a position lying on your back on a flat exercise bench holding a barbell above your shoulders with both arms straight. Your hands should be six to eight inches apart.

Eccentric Phase: Inhale while lowering the bar to the top of your forehead by bending only at the elbows.

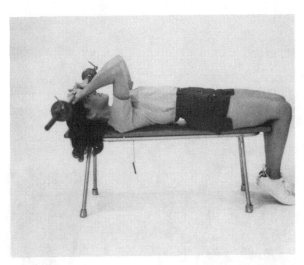

Concentric Phase: Exhale as you push the bar back to the starting position.

Variations: This exercise may also be performed on an incline bench or a decline bench. There are several variations of this exercise using one or two dumbbells.

STANDING TRICEP EXTENSION

Muscles Developed: Triceps.

Starting Position: Start in a standing position with both hands holding one dumbbell overhead.

Eccentric Phase: Inhale as you lower the weight behind your head.

Concentric Phase: Exhale as you extend both arms and push the weight back to the starting position.

Variations: This exercise may also be performed with a barbell as well as in a sitting position.

Additional Information: Keep the elbows up throughout the exercise.

ARM (FOREARM)

BARBELL WRIST CURL

Muscles Developed: Wrist and hand flexors.

Starting Position: Start in a position sitting on an exercise bench with both forearms also on the bench and the hands extended beyond the end of the bench. Hold a barbell with a supinated grip (thumbs out) and allow the bar to hang toward the floor.

Concentric Phase: Exhale as you raise the weight moving only at the wrist joint.

Eccentric Phase: Inhale as the bar is lowered to the starting position.

Variations: This exercise may also be performed using one dumbbell in each hand or using one dumbbell and exercising one arm at a time.

REVERSE WRIST CURL

Muscles Developed: Wrist extensors.

Starting Position: Start in a sitting position on an exercise bench with the forearms resting on the top of the thighs and the hands extended beyond the knees. Hold a barbell in both hands using a pronated grip (thumbs in).

Concentric Phase: Exhale while raising the bar as high as possible moving only at the wrist joint.

Eccentric Phase: Inhale while lowering the bar to the starting position.

Variations: Variations of this exercise may be performed by placing the forearms across an exercise bench or by using dumbbells.

LEG (UPPER LEG)

SQUAT

Muscles Developed: Quadriceps, gluteus maximus, hamstrings.

Starting Position: Start in a standing position with a barbell across the shoulders and upper back.

Eccentric Phase: Inhale as you bend your knees and hips while keeping your head up and your back flat. Continue bending the knees and hips until the thighs are parallel to the floor.

Concentric Phase: Exhale as you straighten your legs and hips to return to a standing position.

Spotting: This exercise should be performed with one spotter standing directly behind the performer or with two spotters, one at each end of the bar. If no spotters are available, squats may be performed in the type of squat rack that ensures that you will not get stuck at the bottom of the exercise under a heavy barbell.

Additional Information: This exercise is often performed with a two-inch block under the heels to help maintain a fairly erect posture in the back while performing the exercise.

FRONT SQUAT

Muscles Developed: Quadriceps, gluteus.

Starting Position: Start in a standing position with a barbell supported across the top of the chest and shoulders. Hold the bar at shoulder level with both hands. Keep the elbows high.

Eccentric Phase: Inhale as you bend your knees and hips until the thighs are parallel to the floor.

Concentric Phase: Exhale as you return to a standing position.

Spotting: One spotter at each end of the bar would be best. If training alone, a person could perform front squats in a squat rack on which the weight could be placed at the bottom of this lift if it is not possible to return to a standing position.

LUNGE

Muscles Developed: Quadriceps, gluteus.

Starting Position: Start in a standing position with a barbell across the shoulders and upper back.

Eccentric Phase: Inhale as you take a large step forward with

one leg. Bend the knee of the lead leg and lower your body until the thigh of the front leg is parallel to the floor. (This is essentially a one-leg parallel squat.)

Concentric Phase: Exhale as you extend your forward leg, pushing yourself back to the original standing position.

Spotting: One spotter at each end of the bar works very well. If you train alone, perform the lunge into a squat rack that could support the weight if you are unable to return to the standing position.

Additional Information: Keep your head up and upper body erect throughout the exercise.

LEG (LOWER LEG)

STANDING BARBELL CALF RAISE

Muscles Developed: Gastrocnemius, soleus.

Starting Position: Start in a standing position with a barbell across the shoulders and upper back. The front half of both feet should be elevated so that the heels are lower than the toes.

Concentric Phase: Exhale while moving only at the ankle joint to raise your heels as high as possible. Pause briefly at the highest position.

Eccentric Phase: Inhale as you lower both heels as far as they can go. The best stretch and maximum range of motion are achieved if the heels cannot touch the floor.

Additional Information: It is difficult to maintain balance during this exercise. Performing this exercise in a power rack or on a standing calf raise machine will generally increase the effectiveness of the exercise, since the balance problem can then be eliminated.

ONE DUMBBELL CALF RAISE

Muscles Developed: Gastrocnemius, soleus.

Starting Position: Start in a standing position holding a dumbbell in one hand hanging at arms length and resting against the side of the thigh. Place all of your body weight on the leg nearest the dumbbell and lift the other foot off of the ground. Brace the free foot against the back of the support leg so that you do not use a kicking motion of that leg to help lift the weight.

Concentric Phase: Exhale as you raise the heel of the support foot at high as possible. Pause at the top.

Eccentric Phase: Inhale as you slowly lower the heel of the supporting foot to a fully stretched position.

Additional Information: The hand that is not holding the dumbbell should be placed on a wall or some other solid support for balance. Use the support hand for balance only; do not pull with that arm to help lift the weight.

DONKEY CALF RAISE

Muscles Developed: Gastrocnemius, soleus.

Starting Position: Start with your legs straight, bend forward at the waist, and place your hands on a bench. Position the feet so that the front half of each foot is on a raised block. Have a training partner sit on top of your hips, not on your lower back.

Concentric Phase: Exhale as the heels are raised as high as possible. Pause at the top.

Eccentric Phase: Inhale as the heels are lowered to a fully stretched position.

Additional Information: This exercise eliminates the balance problem of standing barbell calf raises but makes it difficult to accurately control progressive gains in resistance.

CHAPTER 12

Universal Exercises

Weight stack machines provide safety, ease of weight change, and ease of learning exercises but limit the number of variations of each exercise that barbells and dumbbells offer. However, the basic exercises that are the core of any weight training program may be performed without a spotter.

This chapter in arranged in the following order.

Chest
  Bench Press
  Parallel Bar Dips

Back (Upper Back)
  Shoulder Shrug

Back (Lower Back)
  Back Extension

Back (Middle Outer Back)
  Lat Pull
  Pulley Rowing

Shoulders
  Seated Press
  Press Behind the Neck

Arm (Elbow Flexion)
  Low Pulley Curl

Arm (Elbow Extension)
  Tricep Pressdown

Arm (Forearm)
  Wrist Roller
  Hand Gripper

Leg (Upper Leg)
  Leg Press
  Leg Extension
  Leg Curl

Leg (Lower Leg)
  Calf Press
  Calf Raise (Bench Press Station)
  Calf Raise (Calf Raise Machine)

CONCENTRIC AND ECCENTRIC PHASES

The concentric and eccentric phases of a weight training exercise are explained on the first page of Chapter 11.

CHEST

BENCH PRESS

Muscles Developed: Pectoralis major, anterior deltoid, triceps.

Starting Position: Start in a position lying on your back on a flat bench. Place your head toward the weight stack with the bench press bar above the chest.

Concentric Phase: Exhale as you press the weight upward until your arms are straight.

Eccentric Phase: Inhale as you lower the weight to the starting position.

PARALLEL BAR DIPS

Muscles Developed: Triceps, pectoralis major, anterior deltoid.

Starting Position: Start in a straight arm support position on two bars that are parallel to each other and about shoulder width apart.

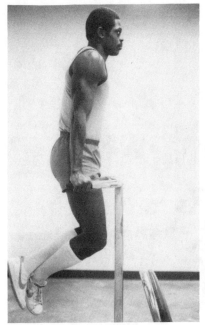 

Eccentric Phase: Inhale as you bend your elbows and slowly lower yourself as far as possible.

Concentric Phase: Exhale as you straighten your arms and return to the starting position.

Additional Information: To add weight to this exercise, hang a weight or a dumbbell from a wide strap around your waist and place it between your thighs to stabilize it during the exercise.

BACK (UPPER BACK)

SHOULDER SHRUG

Muscles Developed: Trapezius.

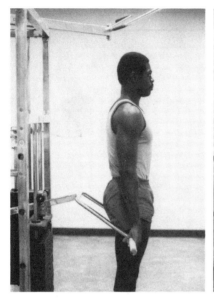 

Starting Position: Start in a standing position at the bench press station holding the bench press bar with a pronated grip (thumbs in) and both arms straight.

Concentric Phase: Inhale as you lift or shrug your shoulders as high as possible.

Eccentric Phase: Exhale as you lower the weight to the starting position.

Variations: (1) Pull your shoulders forward and up, then back and down. (2) Pull your shoulders back and up, then forward and down.

BACK (LOWER BACK)

BACK EXTENSIONS

Muscles Developed: Erector spinae.

Starting Position: Start in a face-down position with your hips supported by a back extension bench. Place your feet in a position to provide stability to the lower body.

Concentric Phase: Inhale as you raise your upper body to a position in which your back is parallel to the floor.

Eccentric Phase: Exhale as you return to the starting position.

Variations: This exercise may also be performed on a flat exercise bench by lying the front of your legs and hips on the bench and your upper body extended beyond the end of the bench. Have someone hold your feet.

Additional Information: This exercise may be performed with your hands placed on your lower back, your arms crossed on your chest, or your hands behind your head. As your arms are moved away from your waist and toward your head, the resistance is increased. To add more resistance, hold a barbell plate behind your neck or on your chest with your arms crossed.

BACK (MIDDLE OUTER BACK)

LAT PULL

Muscles Developed: Latissimus dorsi.

Starting Position: Start in a kneeling or sitting position below

the high pulley station holding the exercise bar with a fairly wide grip and both arms extended.

Concentric Phase: Exhale as you pull the exercise bar to your upper back at the base of the neck.

Eccentric Phase: Inhale as you return to the starting position.

Variations: (1) Pull the exercise bar to the top of your chest. (2) Alternate pulling to the front and to the back. (3) Vary the width of your hand spacing. (4) Change to a supinated grip shoulder width or closer. This is a good way to get strong enough to perform chin ups.

Additional Information: As the weight used for this exercise approaches your body weight, it may be necessary to have someone stand behind you and hold you down.

PULLEY ROWING

Muscles Developed: Latissimus dorsi, trapezius, rear deltoid.

Starting Position: Start in a position sitting on the floor in

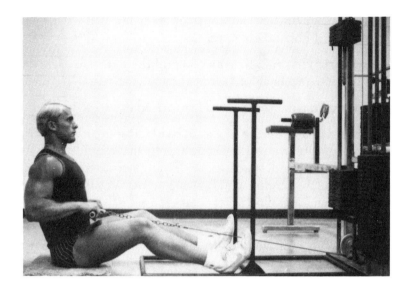

front of the low pulley station of a weight stack machine. Hold the exercise bar in your hands with a pronated grip (thumbs in).

Concentric Phase: Exhale as you pull the exercise bar to the lower portion of the rib cage.

Eccentric Phase: Inhale as you return to the starting position.

Variations: (1) This exercise may also be done in a bent over standing position. (2) Variations of the seated pulley rowing may be achieved by changing grip spacing and by changing the position on the front of the torso toward which the bar is pulled.

SHOULDERS

SEATED PRESS

Muscles Developed: Deltoid, triceps.

Starting Position: Start in a sitting position facing toward the

weight stacked with the exercise bar in line with your shoulders. Place your hands on the exercise bar wider than shoulder width.

Concentric Phase: Inhale as you press the exercise bar upward until your arms are straight.

Eccentric Phase: Exhale as you lower the exercise bar to the starting position.

Additional Information: Try to keep your back straight throughout the exericse; do not arch your back.

PRESS BEHIND THE NECK

Muscles Developed: Deltoid, triceps.

Starting Position: Start in a sitting position facing away from the weight stack. The exercise bar should be approximately in line with the shoulders and the hands should be placed on the bar wider than the shoulders.

Concentric Phase: Inhale as you press the exercise bar upward until your arms are straight.

Eccentric Phase: Exhale as you lower the bar to the starting position.

Additional Information: Try to keep your back straight during the entire exercise. Do not arch your back.

ARM (ELBOW FLEXION)

LOW PULLEY CURL

Muscles Developed: Biceps.

Starting Position: Start in a standing position in front of the low pulley facing toward the weight stack. Hold the exercise bar in a supinated grip (thumbs out) with both arms straight.

Concentric Phase: Exhale as you bend only at the elbow joint to bring the exercise bar up toward your shoulders. Move only your forearms; do not allow your upper arms to change position.

Eccentric Phase: Inhale as you lower the bar to the starting position.

Variations: (1) Change your grip spacing on the bar. (2) Use a pronated grip (thumbs in) and perform reverse curls.

Additional Information: There are a number of ways to cheat on this exercise. Bending any joint except the elbow joint will reduce the effectiveness of the exercise.

ARM (ELBOW EXTENSION)

TRICEP PRESSDOWN

Muscles Developed: Triceps.

Starting Position: Start in a standing position with both hands on the high pulley exercise bar in a pronated grip (thumbs in). Your hands should be slightly closer than shoulder width. Bring the bar down to shoulder level with your elbows bent. Point both elbows directly toward the floor.

Concentric Phase: Exhale as you press the bar down by moving only the forearms. Keep the upper arm in a fixed position throughout the exercise.

Eccentric Phase: Inhale as you allow the bar to return to the starting position. Do not allow your upper arm to change position.

Variations: Grip spacing on this exercise may be changed to result in variations. The grip may vary from hands together to shoulder width apart.

Additional Information: Keep your body still and move only at the elbow joints.

ARM (FOREARM)

WRIST ROLLER

Muscles Developed: Muscles of the forearm, wrist flexors, and extensors, and hand flexors.

Starting Position: Start in a standing position in front of the wrist roller attachment. Place both hands on the wrist roller in a pronated grip (thumbs in).

Concentric Phase: Start with the wrist of one hand in full hyperextension so that the wrist is lower than the hand. Grip the wrist roller and rotate it to full flexion so that the wrist is above the hand. Repeat this movement with the other hand. Continue to alternate hands until the repetitions are completed.

Variations: (1) Reverse the motion so that you start with one wrist in complete flexion (wrist above hand) and rotate the wrist roller to complete wrist hyperextension (wrist below hand). (2) Use a supinated grip (thumbs out).

HAND GRIPPERS

Muscles Developed: Hand flexors.

Starting Position: Start in a standing position in front of the hand grip attachment. Place both hands on the exercise equipment.

Concentric Phase: Pull with the fingers of one hand until the gripper can go no further. Pull with the fingers of the other hand until the gripper can travel no further. Continue to alternate hands until your repetitions are completed.

Variations: (1) Change to a supinated grip (thumbs out).

LEG (UPPER LEG)

LEG PRESS

Muscles Developed: Quadriceps, some gluteus maximus.

Starting Position: Start in a sitting position on the leg press station. Place both feet on the foot pedals. Adjust the seat so that there is an angle of about ninety degrees at the knee joint.

Concentric Phase: Exhale as you push on the foot pedals and straighten both legs.

Eccentric Phase: Inhale as you allow the weight to return to the starting position.

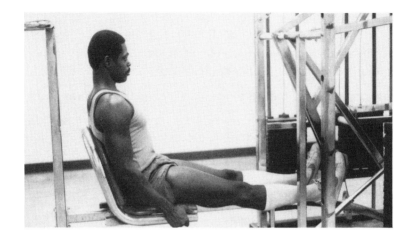

LEG EXTENSION

Muscles Developed: Quadriceps.

Starting Position: Start in a sitting position on the leg extension machine with both feet behind the padded leg extension bar.

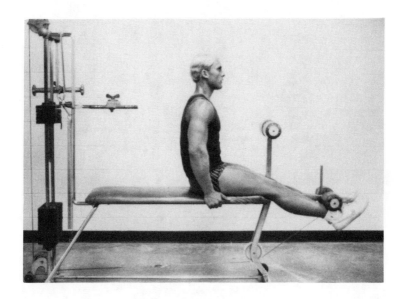

Concentric Phase: Exhale as you extend both legs until they are straight.

Eccentric Phase: Inhale as you allow the weight to return to the starting position.

Variations: On some leg extension machines it is possible to perform this exercise with one leg at a time.

LEG CURL

Muscles Developed: Hamstrings.

Starting Position: Start in a position lying face down on the leg curl machine. With your legs straight, place both feet under the padded leg curl bar.

Concentric Phase: Exhale as you pull both feet toward the hips, bending only at the knees.

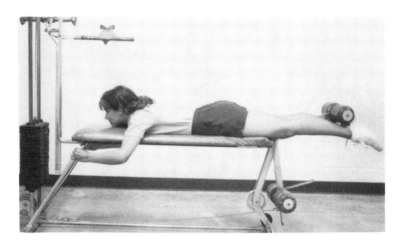

Eccentric Phase: Inhale as you allow the weight to return to the starting position.

Variations: Exercise one leg at a time.

LEG (LOWER LEG)

CALF PRESS

Muscles Developed: Gastrocnemius, soleus.

Starting Position: Start in a sitting position on the leg press

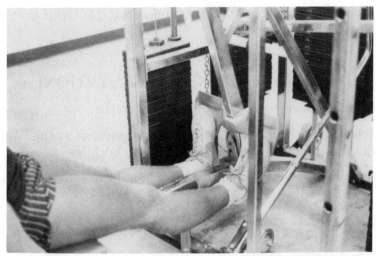

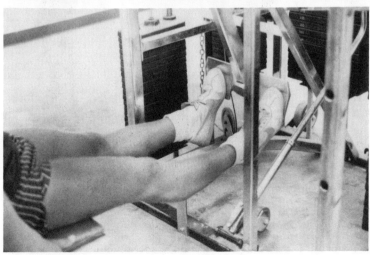

station with both legs straight and the front half of each foot on the pedals. The back half of each foot should extend beyond the bottom of the pedals.

Concentric Phase: Exhale as you press against the pedals with the front portion of your feet. Move only at the ankle joint.

Eccentric Phase: Inhale as you allow the foot pedals to return to the starting position.

Variations: (1) Toes turned in, heels out. (2) Heels in, toes turned out.

CALF RAISE (BENCH PRESS STATION)

Muscles Developed: Gastrocnemius, soleus.

Starting Position: Start in a standing position at the bench press station. Hold the exercise bar with both hands.

Concentric Phase: Exhale while raising the weight by moving only at the ankle joint.

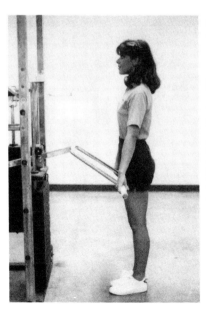 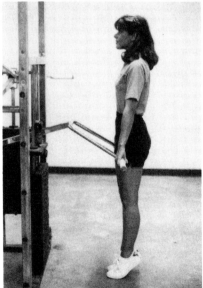

Eccentric Phase: Inhale while slowly returning to the starting position.

Variations: (1) Feet parallel. (2) Toes in. (3) Toes out.

Additional Information: This exercise is more effective when the front half of the foot is placed on an elevated surface such as a block of wood.

CALF RAISE (CALF RAISE MACHINE)

Muscles Developed: Gastrocnemius, soleus.

Starting Position: Start in a standing position with your shoulders under the padded bars of the calf machine. The front half of each foot should be on the elevated block and the heels should be below that level.

Concentric Phase: Exhale as you raise the weight, moving only at the ankle joint.

Eccentric Phase: Inhale as you return to the starting position.

Variations: (1) Feet parallel. (2) Toes in. (3) Toes out.

CHAPTER 13

Abdominal Exercises

The abdominal muscles extend from the lower portion of the rib cage to the upper portion of the hip bones and cover the lower half of the front of the torso. Any time this distance is shortened against resistance, the abdominal muscles are exercised. Also, any time the hip or chest is stabilized and the other portion is twisted, the abdominal obliques are exercised. Keeping that in mind, it is possible to understand that there are many variations of abdominal exercises.

CRUNCHES

Muscles Developed: Abdominals.

Starting Position: Start in a position lying on your back on the floor or an exercise mat. Place your lower legs on a bench and your hands behind your head.

Concentric Phase: Exhale as you lift your head, neck, shoulders, and upper back off of the floor in that order. Keep your lower back on the floor throughout the exercise. Gently curl up to this position using the abdominal muscles. At the upper limit of this movement, pause for one or two seconds with the abdominals fully contracted.

Eccentric Phase: Inhale as you reverse the curling motion and return to the starting position.

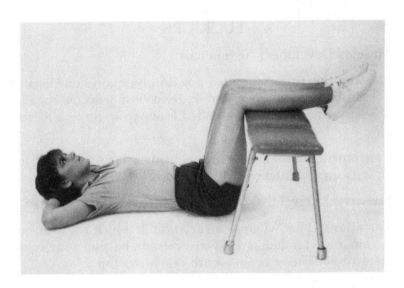

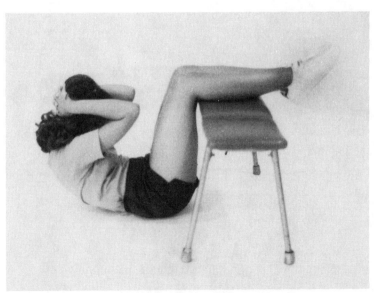

Variations: One variation is to keep the legs straight and place the back side of the legs against a wall. If you wish to add weight to this exercise, place it on the upper chest and hold it there by crossing your arms on top of the weight and your chest.

TUCK UPS

Muscles Developed: Abdominals.

Starting Position: Start in a position lying on your back on the floor or on an exercise mat. Extend your arms overhead so that your entire body is extended from your fingers to your toes.

Concentric Phase: Exhale as you bring your upper body and your legs up to a tucked sitting position.

Eccentric Phase: Inhale as you return to the starting position.

Variations: The "V" up is a variation in which the arms and legs remain extended as they are raised and you touch your fingers to your toes as they both reach the top.

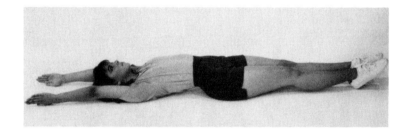

CURL UPS

Muscles Developed: Abdominals.

Starting Position: Start in a position lying on your back on the floor or on an exercise mat with your knees bent, both feet flat on the floor, and your arms crossed on your chest with each hand touching the opposite shoulder.

Concentric Phase: Exhale as you bring your head, neck, shoulders, upper back, and lower back off of the floor in that order.

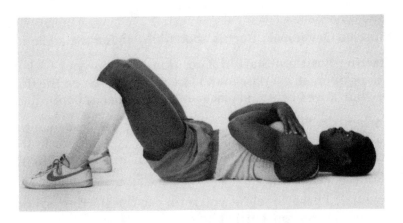

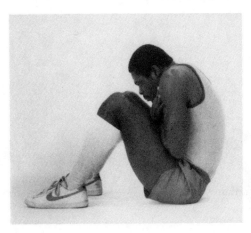

Eccentric Phase: Inhale as you return to the starting position, slowly placing the lower back, upper back, shoulders, neck, and head back on the floor in that order.

Variations: Variations of this exercise are created by changing your arm position or adding weight. If weight is added, place it on your upper chest and hold it in place with your hands. As weight is added, you will probably need to anchor your feet by placing them under something or by having someone hold them.

TWISTING SIT UPS

Muscles Developed: Rectus abdominis, abdominal obliques.

Starting Position: Start in a position lying on your back on the floor or on an exercise mat. Place your feet flat on the floor with your knees bent and place your hands behind your head.

Concentric Phase: Exhale as you bring your head, neck, shoulders, upper back, and lower back off of the floor in that order, twisting as you come up. Touch one elbow to the opposite knee.

Eccentric Phase: Inhale as you return to the starting position by reversing the concentric phase.

Variations: (1) The arm position may be changed. (2) Weight may be added on the upper chest or behind the head.

Additional Information: Alternate the direction of the twist on each repetition.

SEATED TWISTING

Muscles Developed: Abdominal obliques.

Starting Position: Start in a position sitting on an exercise bench with one leg on each side of the bench to stabilize your hips during this exercise. Place a bar on your shoulders and upper back. Straighten your arms along the bar.

Concentric Phase: Exhale as you turn your shoulders and chest as far as possible.

Eccentric Phase: Inhale as you return to the starting position.

Variations: (1) Hold a weight in both hands in front of your body at waist level and twist. (2) From a standing position with a

bar on your shoulders, bend at the waist so that your back is parallel to the floor, then twist.

Additional Information: Alternate the direction of the twist with each repetition.

LYING KNEE UPS

Muscles Developed: Abdominals.

Starting Position: Start in a position lying on your back on the floor, an exercise mat, a sit up board, or an exercise bench. Your legs should be extended.

Concentric Phase: Exhale as you pull your knees toward your shoulders.

Eccentric Phase: Inhale as you return to the starting position.

Additional Information: This exercise is sometimes referred to as a reverse sit up, since the upper body is stabilized and the lower body moves.

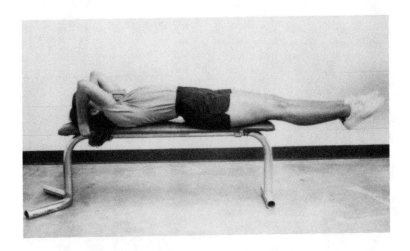

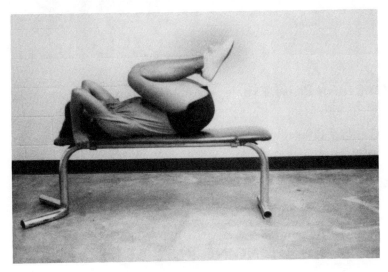

SEATED KNEE UPS

Muscles Developed: Abdominals.

Starting Position: Start in a sitting position on the edge of a bench or chair. Lean back with your shoulders, straighten your legs, and lift both feet off of the floor.

Concentric Phase: Exhale as you bring your knees up toward your shoulders.

Eccentric Phase: Inhale as you return your legs to the starting position.

HANGING KNEE UPS

Muscles Developed: Abdominals.

Starting Position: Start in a position in which you are hanging from your hands.

Concentric Phase: Exhale as you bring your knees up toward your shoulders.

Eccentric Phase: Inhale as you return your legs to the starting position.

CHAPTER 14

Rest, Nutrition, and Drugs

Without adequate rest and nutrition your weight training progress will be slow. Weight training exercise is the stimulus, but the positive changes that occur in the muscular system as a result take place between exercise sessions as your body rebuilds and attempts to adapt to the exercise overload.

REST

Weight training progress is best when a muscle receives two to four days rest between exercise sessions. Less than two days rest or more than four days rest between exercise sessions results in slower progress.

An average amount of sleep is eight hours per night. However, sleep requirements vary from one person to another, and for the same person based upon changes in their activity levels. Beginning weight trainers may initially find that they need to sleep more to recover from this new demand. As they become accustomed to the increased physical activity and their bodies begin to function more efficiently, they often return to normal sleep patterns. "Hard-gainers," individuals who have a very hard time gaining muscle, sometimes need as much as ten hours sleep each night. Some "easy gainers" or natural mesomorphs may gain on seven hours sleep per night. Very few individuals progress well on less than seven hours sleep per night. This is often one of the greatest training problems for the young adults (age 16 to 30) who have the greatest potential for weight training development. Many high school students, college students, and young single adults train hard with weights but do not get enough sleep to fully recover from their training sessions.

Weight training is very intense and demanding. Too many other physical activities will also slow your weight training progress. If you wish to maximize your weight training gains, cut down on your other physically strenuous activities. Once again, it is generally the young adults (ages 16 to 30) who wear themselves out with a large number of activities.

The combination of too much activity and not enough rest can cancel out all of the hard work you put into your weight training exercises.

Some experienced weight trainers believe that they progress better if they train hard for six to eight weeks, take one week off, then start a new training program.

As you get older, some of your bodily functions begin to slow down. Beyond an approximate age of forty, it may be that two workouts per week will be sufficient. However, it will depend on your weight training goals and your personal ability to recover from your workouts.

Some days you feel better than others. There will undoubtedly be days that you will not feel up to your normal workout. On those days it is generally best to train anyway but reduce your intensity and your total workload to a level that feels good. Do not skip your workout completely. Maintain your frequency of workouts. Once you skip a training session, it is very easy to skip another and another. Soon you have no training schedule at all. It is very easy to stop training completely and very difficult to get started again. It is safe to say that many will begin weight training, but few will have what it takes to continue. Persistence is a common word but a rare human quality.

The only time you should not train is when you are sick. If you are truly physically sick, you should not work out, because it will further stress your body. It is not possible to "sweat out" a cold or any other illness. See your doctor, follow his advice, get in bed, and rest completely so that you can get well in the shortest possible time. If you keep training, an illness can drag on for weeks, and you will probably not experience any progress in spite of your training efforts. Weight training should contribute to your health. When you are not well, stop training and get well, then start again. If you get sick more than once or twice a year, you should examine your life-style. It is probably not a very healthy one.

If you feel exhausted when you wake up and are sleepy all day long, even during activities you normally enjoy, you may not be getting enough rest. If you are sleeping about eight hours each night and are still feeling tired, you may be overtraining. Try reducing the total number of sets in your weight training program, and see if you feel better.

Adequate rest and recovery time are essential to your weight training progress.

NUTRITION

There are six classes of nutrients that your body needs to function properly.

Water
Minerals
Vitamins
Carbohydrates
Fats
Proteins

WATER. Water provides no calories or vitamins but is essential in relatively large quantities for the human body to function properly. When you are thirsty, your body is asking for water. What do you give it?

It is almost impossible to drink too much water. If you do take in more water than you need, your body can easily get rid of the excess. If you do not take in enough water, your body cannot continue to function normally, and your performance will suffer.

MINERALS. Minerals are inorganic substances that are

necessary for some of the chemical activity that goes on in your body. If the appropriate minerals are not present, certain chemical changes cannot occur.

VITAMINS. Vitamins are organic substances that are necessary for some of the chemical activity that goes on in your body. They are necessary for tissue building, the release of energy, and for controlling the body's use of food. There are two major categories of vitamins—fat soluble (A, D, E, K) and water soluble (all others). Fat soluble vitamins can be stored in the body, and it is possible to take too much of those vitamins. Excess water soluble vitamins are generally excreted in the urine.

There is a need for adequate amounts of water, minerals, and vitamins. In each case, a deficiency will decrease optimal bodily function and performance. However, more than the required amount will not improve performance or progress. A good guideline to follow is to eat a balanced diet from a variety of good foods and to drink water whenever you are thirsty.

Calories (body fuel) are contained in carbohydrates, fats, and proteins.

CARBOHYDRATES. Carbohydrates are a major source of energy for your body, particularly during high intensity exercise.

FATS. Fats have a higher energy value than carbohydrates, providing up to 70 percent of your total body energy when you are in a resting state or during low-level physical activity. They also serve as an essential component of cell walls and nerve fibers. Fats are involved in the absorption and transport of fat soluble vitamins. While fats are very useful in your body, it is possible to have too much of a good thing. What you need is the right amount of fat in your diet. Do not cut fats out of your diet completely or eat too many fats—either extreme can be detrimental.

PROTEINS. Proteins are complex organic compounds made up of amino acids. Proteins are essential for growth and repair of your body tissues. Proteins are a potential source of energy but are generally spared when fats and carbohydrates are available in ample supply.

Twenty-two amino acids have been identified. Nine of these amino acids are essential in your diet. If any one of the amino acids is missing, your body cannot put together all of the protein structures that it needs.

Carbohydrates, fats, and proteins are all necessary in your food intake. In each case, a deficiency creates a problem, an adequate amount is optimal, and more is not better. The suggested caloric intake balance for adults is as follows:

50-55 percent Carbohydrates
30-35 percent Fats
10-20 percent Proteins

THE "SECRET" WEIGHT TRAINING DIET

Many weight trainers and athletes are looking for the secret or magic diet or food that will make them a great success. The truth is that there is no one food or diet that can do that. The closest thing to a secret or magic diet is a balanced diet that includes all of the nutrients your body needs in the correct amounts. The only difference between the diet that is best for the average sedentary adult and the diet that is best for the active athlete or weight trainer might be the total number of calories consumed. The athlete or weight trainer may use more total calories because of greater energy expenditure. This secret diet should include a wide variety of good quality food in the proper amounts. You must eat right to gain healthy muscle tissue and remove excess stored body fat. Carbonated drinks and chips will not result in quality muscle tissue but certainly can be stored as fat. It is important to get the highly processed junk food out of your diet and eat high quality good food. You need to learn to tell the difference. Some of the top body builders claim that their body building success may be as much as 80 percent due to nutrition.

Grain

Group

Carbohydrate
Thiamin (B$_1$)
Iron
Niacin

4 Servings

Whole grain, fortified, or
enriched grain products
are recommended.

OAT
cereal

FOOD GROUP PLAN. One easy way to balance all of those nutritional requirements is to follow the food group plan.

FOOD GROUP AND AMOUNT

Grains (Breads and Cereals)
   4 or more servings per day

Fruits and Vegetables
   4 or more servings per day

Meats
   2 or more servings per day

Milk (Dairy Products)
   2 or more servings per day

FOOD SUPPLEMENTS. If you are eating a balanced diet of good quality foods, there appears to be no need for food supplements. There is no miracle food or magic food that will make your muscles grow. Independent researchers (those who don't sell food supplements) have found no benefit results from protein supplements or vitamin supplements when subjects are on a balanced diet.

WEIGHT GAIN. To gain muscular body weight, perform brief heavy weight training exercise. Work the largest muscle groups and eat a balanced diet of good quality food. Increase your total caloric intake by 500 to 1,000 calories per day. Eat more frequently, but eat smaller meals and get plenty of rest. Slow down, stay calm, and decrease your other physical activities.

WEIGHT LOSS. When you start a weight training program, you will gain muscle and lose fat. It is difficult to experience any significant loss in total body weight until muscle growth slows down. However, to lose fat perform longer training sessions (burn more calories). Continuous, rhythmic activities that use large muscle groups are best. Examples of good weight loss activities are walking, swimming, cycling, and jogging. Eat a

Fruit- Vegetable

4 Servings

Group

Vitamins A and C

Dark green, leafy, or orange vegetables and fruit are recommended 3 or 4 times weekly for vitamin A. Citrus fruit is recommended daily for vitamin C.

meat
Group

Protein
Niacin
Iron
Thiamin (B₁)

2 Servings

Dry beans and peas, soy extenders, and nuts combined with animal protein (meat, fish, poultry, eggs, milk, cheese) or grain protein can be substituted for a serving of meat.

balanced diet of good quality food. Do not skip meals or omit any particular good group. Decrease your total caloric intake by 500 to 1,000 calories per day. Participate in more physical activities, and select activities in which food is not easily available. Try getting less rest and sleep. You do not burn calories very fast when you are sleeping.

DRUGS, ALCOHOL, AND TOBACCO

ANABOLIC STEROIDS. Anabolic steriods present the biggest drug problem in weight training. Anabolic steroids are synthetic compounds that are like the natural hormones produced by your body. They are thought to promote muscular growth. Steroids have been difficult to study because they have highly undesirable and dangerous side effects. Therefore, they can be studied only at safe (low) levels. The athletes who claim that steroids work take massive doses that are ten to twenty times greater than the safe dose a physician would allow in a research study.

Some of the undesirable side effects that have been observed are: endocrine disturbances, atrophy of the testicles, male impotency, liver damage, and possible liver cancer.

All steroid users agree that steroids only work when accompanied by extremely hard weight training. Therefore, steroids are not a "miracle drug" and "easy gain" muscle drug that replaces hard work. Very intense workouts are necessary. This is another reason why steroids are hard to study. It is difficult to determine how much of the improvement was due to the extremely hard training and how much might have been due to the steroid effect.

Many steroid users report an increase in aggressiveness. This increased aggressiveness during weight training workouts could result in more intense workouts and greater gains by itself.

At any rate, anabolic steroids do not have proven value in increasing weight training progress and do have dangerous side effects. The use of steroids will also result in disqualification from top quality lifting competitions.

Some young lifters and body builders are suffering irreparable lifelong damage to their bodies, and there have been some deaths attributed to steroid use. Competition has perhaps become unfair for the small percentage that don't abuse steroids. Weight training should improve your health and natural performance level. Drug abuse has no place in a health development program.

ALCOHOL. There is no evidence that light to moderate alcohol consumption interferes with weight training progress. Heavy alcohol consumption has a very profound and obvious detrimental effect on the human body.

TOBACCO. Smoking or chewing tobacco has no known beneficial effects. Smoking tobacco has proven harmful on the respiratory and circulatory systems. Smoking decreases your performance capability and training capacity. It not only reduces your ability to put in long hard workouts, but it also interferes with your ability to relax and sleep.

References

Allsen, Philip E. *Fitness for Life: An Individualized Approach.* Dubuque, Iowa: Wm. C. Brown Publishers, 1984.

Astrand, Per-Olof and Kaare Rodahl. *Textbook of Work Physiology.* New York, N.Y.: McGraw-Hill Book Company, 1977.

Berger, Richard A. *Introduction to Weight Training.* Englewood Cliffs, N.J.: Prentice-Hall, Inc., 1984.

Cook, Brian and Gordon W. Stewart. *Get Strong.* Ganges, British Columbia, Canada: 3 S Fitness Group, 1981.

Corbin, Charles B., Linus J. Dowell, Ruth Lindsey, and Homer Tolson. *Concepts in Physical Education.* Dubuque, Iowa: Wm. C. Brown Company Publishers, 1981.

deVries, Herbert A. *Physiology of Exercise.* Dubuque, Iowa: Wm. C. Brown Company Publishers, 1980.

Epley, Boyd and Tom Wilson. *Weight Training Instruction Manual.* Lincoln, Nebraska: Body Enterprises, 1981.

Ferrigno, Lou and Douglas Kent Hall. *The Incredible Lou Ferrigno.* New York, N.Y.: Simon and Schuster, 1982.

Hatfield, Frederick C. and March L. Krotee. *Personalized Weight Training for Fitness and Athletics.* Dubuque, Iowa: Kendall/Hunt Publishing Company, 1978.

Hesson, James L. *A Formula for Success.* Unpublished research material, 1980.

O'Shea, John Patrick. *Scientific Principles and Methods of Strength Fitness.* Reading, Mass.: Addison-Wesley Publishing Company, 1976.

Rasch, Philip J. *Weight Training.* Dubuque, Iowa: Wm. C. Brown Company Publishers, 1982.

Riley, Daniel P. and James A. Peterson. *Not for Men Only: Strength Training for Women.* West Point, N.Y.: Leisure Press, 1981.

Riley, Daniel P. *Strength Training by the Experts.* West Point, N.Y.: Leisure Press, 1982.

Sprague, Ken and Bill Reynolds. *The Gold's Gym Book of Bodybuilding*. Chicago: Contemporary Books, Inc., 1983.

Tuten, Rich, Clancy Moore and Virgil Knight. *Weight Training Everyone*. Winston-Salem, N.C.: Hunter Textbooks, Inc., 1983.

Westcott, Wayne L. *Strength Fitness*. Boston: Allyn and Bacon, Inc., 1983.

Wilmore, Jack H. *Training for Sport and Activity*. Boston: Allyn and Bacon, Inc., 1982.

Appendices

Muscle Structure

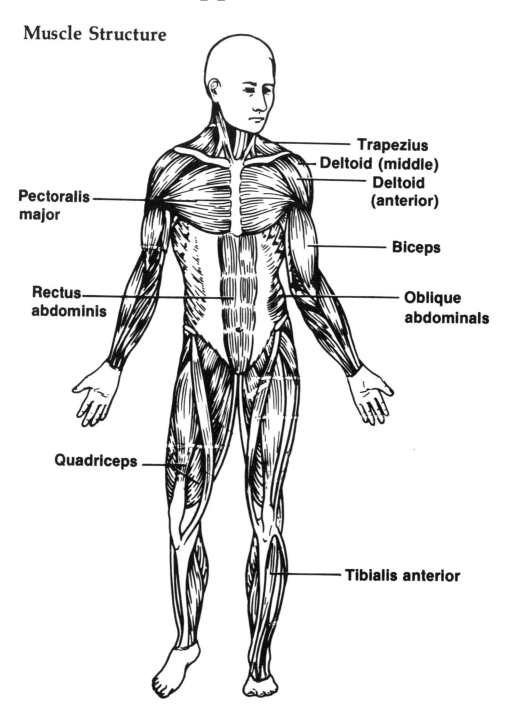

Trapezius
Deltoid (middle)
Deltoid (anterior)
Pectoralis major
Biceps
Rectus abdominis
Oblique abdominals
Quadriceps
Tibialis anterior

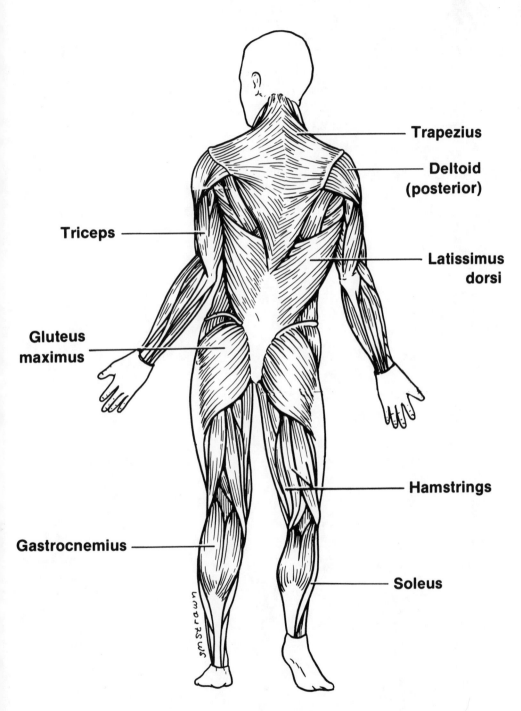

Trapezius

Deltoid (posterior)

Triceps

Latissimus dorsi

Gluteus maximus

Hamstrings

Gastrocnemius

Soleus

Redrawn from F.D. Giddings, 1980.

Name: _____

Section: _____

Goal Setting

Directions:

1. Read Chapter 7, **Goal Setting**.
2. Your weight training goals need to be specific, measurable, believable, and compatible.
3. You need to set a specific date by which you will reach your goal.
4. The goals you choose must be **your** goals. They must be something that you want very much. The greater your desire for the goal, the greater your chance of achieving it.
5. Appropriate weight training goals include changes in muscular strength, size, or endurance.
6. Write at least one, but not more than three, personal weight training goals. These should be short-term goals that can be reached in the next three months.

Goal 1: _____

_____

_____

_____

Goal 2: _____

_____

_____

Goal 3: _____

_____

_____

_____

Name: _____

Section: _____

Planning Your Personal Weight Training Program

Directions:

1. Read Chapter 9, **Guidelines for Planning A Weight Training Program**.
2. Plan an exercise program that is consistent with your goals.
3. Refer to Chapters 11, 12, and 13 for specific exercises.

Body Part	Exercise	Resistance % of 1 RM	Repetitions	Sets	Rest Interval	Frequency Days/wk.

Name: _____

Section: _____

Strength Measurement

Directions:
1. Read Chapter 8, **Record Keeping and Progress**.
2. Train with weights for at least two weeks before testing strength.
3. Test your strength every three or four weeks after the first test.
4. Move the weight in a smooth, continuous manner.
5. Maintain strict exercise form.
6. Do **not** hold your breath.
7. Increase the weight for each set.
8. Rest two minutes between sets.
9. Rest three to five minutes before your final record attempt.
10. The first time you test your strength you will not know your 1 RM. Start with a light weight that you can lift 10 times. After that first warm up set, continue raising the weight and performing one repetition until you reach your one repetition maximum (1 RM).

Strength Test	1st	2nd	3rd	4th
Date				
Exercise_____	Wt	Wt	Wt	Wt
10 reps with 60% of 1 RM				
1 rep with 80% of 1 RM				
1 rep with 85% of 1 RM				
1 rep with 90% of 1 RM				
1 rep with 95% of 1 RM				
1 rep with 102-105% of 1 RM				

Name: _____

Section: _____

Strength Measurement

Directions:
1. Read Chapter 8, **Record Keeping and Progress**.
2. Train with weights for at least two weeks before testing strength.
3. Test your strength every three or four weeks after the first test.
4. Move the weight in a smooth, continuous manner.
5. Maintain strict exercise form.
6. Do **not** hold your breath.
7. Increase the weight for each set.
8. Rest two minutes between sets.
9. Rest three to five minutes before your final record attempt.
10. The first time you test your strength you will not know your 1 RM. Start with a light weight that you can lift 10 times. After that first warm up set, continue raising the weight and performing one repetition until you reach your one repetition maximum (1 RM).

Strength Test	1st	2nd	3rd	4th
Date				
Exercise_____	Wt	Wt	Wt	Wt
10 reps with 60% of 1 RM				
1 rep with 80% of 1 RM				
1 rep with 85% of 1 RM				
1 rep with 90% of 1 RM				
1 rep with 95% of 1 RM				
1 rep with 102-105% of 1 RM				

Name: _____

Section: _____

Strength Measurement

Directions:

1. Read Chapter 8, **Record Keeping and Progress**.
2. Train with weights for at least two weeks before testing strength.
3. Test your strength every three or four weeks after the first test.
4. Move the weight in a smooth, continuous manner.
5. Maintain strict exercise form.
6. Do **not** hold your breath.
7. Increase the weight for each set.
8. Rest two minutes between sets.
9. Rest three to five minutes before your final record attempt.
10. The first time you test your strength you will not know your 1 RM. Start with a light weight that you can lift 10 times. After that first warm up set, continue raising the weight and performing one repetition until you reach your one repetition maximum (1 RM).

Strength Test	1st	2nd	3rd	4th
Date				
Exercise_____	Wt	Wt	Wt	Wt
10 reps with 60% of 1 RM				
1 rep with 80% of 1 RM				
1 rep with 85% of 1 RM				
1 rep with 90% of 1 RM				
1 rep with 95% of 1 RM				
1 rep with 102-105% of 1 RM				

Name: _____

Section: _____

Strength Measurement

Directions:
1. Read Chapter 8, **Record Keeping and Progress**.
2. Train with weights for at least two weeks before testing strength.
3. Test your strength every three or four weeks after the first test.
4. Move the weight in a smooth, continuous manner.
5. Maintain strict exercise form.
6. Do **not** hold your breath.
7. Increase the weight for each set.
8. Rest two minutes between sets.
9. Rest three to five minutes before your final record attempt.
10. The first time you test your strength you will not know your 1 RM. Start with a light weight that you can lift 10 times. After that first warm up set, continue raising the weight and performing one repetition until you reach your one repetition maximum (1 RM).

Strength Test	1st	2nd	3rd	4th
Date				
Exercise_____	Wt	Wt	Wt	Wt
10 reps with 60% of 1 RM				
1 rep with 80% of 1 RM				
1 rep with 85% of 1 RM				
1 rep with 90% of 1 RM				
1 rep with 95% of 1 RM				
1 rep with 102-105% of 1 RM				

Name: _____

Section: _____

Strength Measurement

Directions:
1. Read Chapter 8, **Record Keeping and Progress**.
2. Train with weights for at least two weeks before testing strength.
3. Test your strength every three or four weeks after the first test.
4. Move the weight in a smooth, continuous manner.
5. Maintain strict exercise form.
6. Do **not** hold your breath.
7. Increase the weight for each set.
8. Rest two minutes between sets.
9. Rest three to five minutes before your final record attempt.
10. The first time you test your strength you will not know your 1 RM. Start with a light weight that you can lift 10 times. After that first warm up set, continue raising the weight and performing one repetition until you reach your one repetition maximum (1 RM).

Strength Test	1st	2nd	3rd	4th
Date				
Exercise_____	Wt	Wt	Wt	Wt
10 reps with 60% of 1 RM				
1 rep with 80% of 1 RM				
1 rep with 85% of 1 RM				
1 rep with 90% of 1 RM				
1 rep with 95% of 1 RM				
1 rep with 102-105% of 1 RM				

Name: _____

Section: _____

Strength Measurement

Directions:
1. Read Chapter 8, **Record Keeping and Progress**.
2. Train with weights for at least two weeks before testing strength.
3. Test your strength every three or four weeks after the first test.
4. Move the weight in a smooth, continuous manner.
5. Maintain strict exercise form.
6. Do **not** hold your breath.
7. Increase the weight for each set.
8. Rest two minutes between sets.
9. Rest three to five minutes before your final record attempt.
10. The first time you test your strength you will not know your 1 RM. Start with a light weight that you can lift 10 times. After that first warm up set, continue raising the weight and performing one repetition until you reach your one repetition maximum (1 RM).

Strength Test	1st	2nd	3rd	4th
Date				
Exercise_____	Wt	Wt	Wt	Wt
10 reps with 60% of 1 RM				
1 rep with 80% of 1 RM				
1 rep with 85% of 1 RM				
1 rep with 90% of 1 RM				
1 rep with 95% of 1 RM				
1 rep with 102-105% of 1 RM				

Name: _____

Section: _____

Strength Measurement

Directions:
1. Read Chapter 8, **Record Keeping and Progress**.
2. Train with weights for at least two weeks before testing strength.
3. Test your strength every three or four weeks after the first test.
4. Move the weight in a smooth, continuous manner.
5. Maintain strict exercise form.
6. Do **not** hold your breath.
7. Increase the weight for each set.
8. Rest two minutes between sets.
9. Rest three to five minutes before your final record attempt.
10. The first time you test your strength you will not know your 1 RM. Start with a light weight that you can lift 10 times. After that first warm up set, continue raising the weight and performing one repetition until you reach your one repetition maximum (1 RM).

Strength Test	1st	2nd	3rd	4th
Date				
Exercise_____	Wt	Wt	Wt	Wt
10 reps with 60% of 1 RM				
1 rep with 80% of 1 RM				
1 rep with 85% of 1 RM				
1 rep with 90% of 1 RM				
1 rep with 95% of 1 RM				
1 rep with 102-105% of 1 RM				

Name: _____

Section: _____

Strength Measurement

Directions:
1. Read Chapter 8, **Record Keeping and Progress**.
2. Train with weights for at least two weeks before testing strength.
3. Test your strength every three or four weeks after the first test.
4. Move the weight in a smooth, continuous manner.
5. Maintain strict exercise form.
6. Do **not** hold your breath.
7. Increase the weight for each set.
8. Rest two minutes between sets.
9. Rest three to five minutes before your final record attempt.
10. The first time you test your strength you will not know your 1 RM. Start with a light weight that you can lift 10 times. After that first warm up set, continue raising the weight and performing one repetition until you reach your one repetition maximum (1 RM).

Strength Test	1st	2nd	3rd	4th
Date				
Exercise_____	Wt	Wt	Wt	Wt
10 reps with 60% of 1 RM				
1 rep with 80% of 1 RM				
1 rep with 85% of 1 RM				
1 rep with 90% of 1 RM				
1 rep with 95% of 1 RM				
1 rep with 102-105% of 1 RM				

Name: _____

Section: _____

Size Measurement

Directions:

1. Read Chapter 8, **Record Keeping and Progress**.

Measurement	1st		2nd		3rd		4th	
Date								
Height								
Weight								
Neck (relaxed)								
Shoulders (relaxed)								
Chest (relaxed)								
(flexed)								
Waist (relaxed)								
(flexed)								
Hips (relaxed)								
(flexed)								
Right (R) Left (L)	R	L	R	L	R	L	R	L
Thigh (relaxed)								
(flexed)								
Calf (relaxed)								
(flexed)								
Upper Arm (relaxed)								
(flexed)								
Forearm (relaxed)								
(flexed)								

Name: _____

Section: _____

Muscle Endurance Measurement

Directions:

1. Read Chapter 8, **Record Keeping and Progress**.
2. Test your strength to find your one repetition maximum.
3. Select a weight that is approximately 60% of your 1 RM.
4. Perform as many continuous repetitions as possible. Absolutely **no** rest pause between repetitions.
5. Move the weight in a smooth, controlled manner.
6. Maintain strict exercise form.
7. You may test your muscle endurance every three or four weeks after the first test.
8. Use the same weight for each exercise every time you test yourself for muscle endurance on that exercise. An increase in repetitions using the same weight should indicate an increase in muscle endurance.

Muscle Endurance Test		1st	2nd	3rd	4th
Date					
Exercise	Weight	Reps	Reps	Reps	Reps

Name: _____

Section: _____

Date												
Exercise	Wt	Rep	Wt.	Rep	Wt	Rep	Wt	Rep	Wt	Rep	Wt	Rep

Name: _____

Section: _____

Date												
Exercise	Wt	Rep	Wt.	Rep	Wt	Rep	Wt	Rep	Wt	Rep	Wt	Rep

Name: _____

Section: _____

Date													
Exercise	Wt	Rep	Wt.	Rep	Wt	Rep	Wt	Rep	Wt	Rep	Wt	Rep

Name: _____

Section: _____

Date												
Exercise	Wt	Rep	Wt.	Rep	Wt	Rep	Wt	Rep	Wt	Rep	Wt	Rep

Name: _____

Section: _____

Date												
Exercise	Wt	Rep	Wt.	Rep	Wt	Rep	Wt	Rep	Wt	Rep	Wt	Rep

Name: ———————————————————————

Section: ———————————————————————

Date												
Exercise	Wt	Rep	Wt.	Rep	Wt	Rep	Wt	Rep	Wt	Rep	Wt	Rep

Name: _____

Section: _____

Date													
Exercise	Wt	Rep	Wt.	Rep	Wt	Rep	Wt	Rep	Wt	Rep	Wt	Rep

Name: _____

Section: _____

Date												
Exercise	Wt	Rep	Wt.	Rep	Wt	Rep	Wt	Rep	Wt	Rep	Wt	Rep

Name: _____

Section: _____

Date												
Exercise	Wt	Rep	Wt.	Rep	Wt	Rep	Wt	Rep	Wt	Rep	Wt	Rep

Name: _____

Section: _____

Date												
Exercise	Wt	Rep	Wt.	Rep	Wt	Rep	Wt	Rep	Wt	Rep	Wt	Rep

Name: _____

Section: _____

Date													
Exercise	Wt	Rep	Wt.	Rep	Wt	Rep	Wt	Rep	Wt	Rep	Wt	Rep

Name: ───────────────────────────────

Section: ─────────────────────────────

Date												
Exercise	Wt	Rep	Wt.	Rep	Wt	Rep	Wt	Rep	Wt	Rep	Wt	Rep

Name: _____

Section: _____

Date												
Exercise	Wt	Rep	Wt.	Rep	Wt	Rep	Wt	Rep	Wt	Rep	Wt	Rep

Name: _____

Section: _____

Date												
Exercise	Wt	Rep	Wt.	Rep	Wt	Rep	Wt	Rep	Wt	Rep	Wt	Rep

Index